Windows XP
Top 100
2nd Edition

Simplified®

TIPS & TRICKS

by Paul McFedries

Visual

WILEY

Windows® XP: Top 100 Simplified® Tips & Tricks, 2nd Edition

Published by
Wiley Publishing, Inc.
111 River Street
Hoboken, NJ 07030-5774

Published simultaneously in Canada

Copyright © 2005 by Wiley Publishing, Inc., Indianapolis, Indiana

Library of Congress Control Number: 2005921597

ISBN: 0-7645-8330-1

Manufactured in the United States of America

10 9 8 7 6 5 4 3 2 1

2K/RU/QT/QV/IN

Trademark Acknowledgments

Contact Us

For general information on our other products and services contact our Customer Care Department within the U.S. at 800-762-2974, outside the U.S. at 317-572-3993, or fax 317-572-4002.

For technical support please visit www.wiley.com/techsupport.

Wiley Publishing, Inc.

Sales

Contact Wiley at (800) 762-2974 or fax (317) 572-4002.

PRAISE FOR VISUAL BOOKS

"I have to praise you and your company on the fine products you turn out. I have twelve Visual books in my house. They were instrumental in helping me pass a difficult computer course. Thank you for creating books that are easy to follow. Keep turning out those quality books."
Gordon Justin (Brielle, NJ)

"What fantastic teaching books you have produced! Congratulations to you and your staff. You deserve the Nobel prize in Education. Thanks for helping me understand computers."
Bruno Tonon (Melbourne, Australia)

"A Picture Is Worth A Thousand Words! If your learning method is by observing or hands-on training, this is the book for you!"
Lorri Pegan-Durastante (Wickliffe, OH)

"Over time, I have bought a number of your 'Read Less - Learn More' books. For me, they are THE way to learn anything easily. I learn easiest using your method of teaching."
José A. Mazón (Cuba, NY)

"You've got a fan for life!! Thanks so much!!"
Kevin P. Quinn (Oakland, CA)

"I have several books from the Visual series and have always found them to be valuable resources."
Stephen P. Miller (Ballston Spa, NY)

"I have several of your Visual books and they are the best I have ever used."
Stanley Clark (Crawfordville, FL)

"Like a lot of other people, I understand things best when I see them visually. Your books really make learning easy and life more fun."
John T. Frey (Cadillac, MI)

"I have quite a few of your Visual books and have been very pleased with all of them. I love the way the lessons are presented!"
Mary Jane Newman (Yorba Linda, CA)

"Thank you, thank you, thank you...for making it so easy for me to break into this high-tech world."
Gay O'Donnell (Calgary, Alberta, Canada)

"I write to extend my thanks and appreciation for your books. They are clear, easy to follow, and straight to the point. Keep up the good work! I bought several of your books and they are just right! No regrets! I will always buy your books because they are the best."
Seward Kollie (Dakar, Senegal)

"I would like to take this time to thank you and your company for producing great and easy-to-learn products. I bought two of your books from a local bookstore, and it was the best investment I've ever made! Thank you for thinking of us ordinary people."
Jeff Eastman (West Des Moines, IA)

"Compliments to the chef!! Your books are extraordinary! Or, simply put, extra-ordinary, meaning way above the rest! THANKYOU THANKYOU THANKYOU! I buy them for friends, family, and colleagues."
Christine J. Manfrin (Castle Rock, CO)

CREDITS

Project Editor
Sarah Hellert

Acquisitions Editor
Jody Lefevere

Product Development Manager
Lindsay Sandman

Copy Editor
Scott Tullis

Technical Editor
Don Passenger

Editorial Manager
Robyn Siesky

Editorial Assistant
Adrienne D. Porter

Manufacturing
Allan Conley
Linda Cook
Paul Gilchrist
Jennifer Guynn

Screen Artists
Elizabeth Cardenas-Nelson
Jill A. Proll

Illustrator
Ronda David-Burroughs

Book Design
Kathie Rickard

Production Coordinator
Maridee V. Ennis

Layout
Beth Brooks
Jennifer Heleine
Amanda Spagnuolo

Cover Design
Anthony Bunyan

Proofreader
Sossity R. Smith

Quality Control
John Greenough
Brian H. Walls

Indexer
Johana Van Hoose

Vice President and Executive Group Publisher
Richard Swadley

Vice President and Publisher
Barry Pruett

Composition Services Director
Debbie Stailey

ABOUT THE AUTHOR

Paul McFedries is the president of Logophilia Limited, a technical writing company. Paul has worked with computers large and small since 1975. He has written over 40 books that have sold nearly three million copies worldwide, including the Wiley book *Teach Yourself VISUALLY Windows® XP,* 2nd Edition. Paul is also the proprietor of Word Spy, a Web site devoted to recently coined words and phrases. Word Spy generates over a million page views each month, has won numerous awards, and has been mentioned or featured in publications such as the *New York Times,* the *Wall Street Journal*, and *Time* magazine. Paul invites you to join in the fun at www.wordspy.com.

HOW TO USE THIS BOOK

Windows® XP: Top 100 Simplified® Tips & Tricks includes 100 tasks that reveal cool secrets, teach timesaving tricks, and explain great tips guaranteed to make you more productive with Windows XP. The easy-to-use layout lets you work through all the tasks from beginning to end or jump in at random.

Who Is This Book For?

You already know Windows XP basics. Now you'd like to go beyond, with shortcuts, tricks and tips that let you work smarter and faster. And because you learn more easily when someone *shows* you how, this is the book for you.

Conventions Used In This Book

❶ Steps

This book uses step-by-step instructions to guide you easily through each task. Numbered callouts on every screen shot show you exactly how to perform each task, step by step.

❷ Tips

Practical tips provide insights to save you time and trouble, caution you about hazards to avoid, and reveal how to do things in Windows XP that you never thought possible!

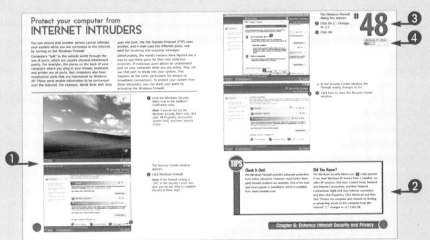

❸ Task Numbers

Task numbers from 1 to 100 indicate which lesson you are working on.

❹ Difficulty Levels

For quick reference, the symbols below mark the difficulty level of each task.

DIFFICULTY LEVEL	Demonstrates a new spin on a common task
DIFFICULTY LEVEL	Introduces a new skill or a new task
DIFFICULTY LEVEL	Combines multiple skills requiring in-depth knowledge
DIFFICULTY LEVEL	Requires extensive skill and may involve other technologies

Table of Contents

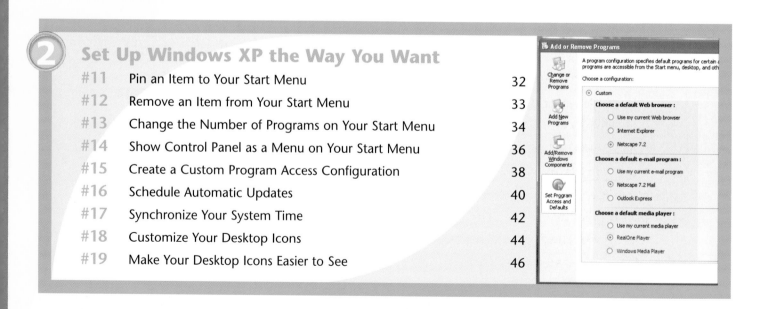

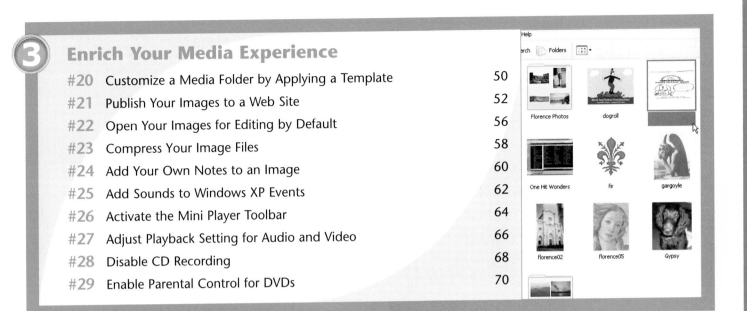

Enrich Your Media Experience

Get the Most Out of Your Files and Folders

Table of Contents

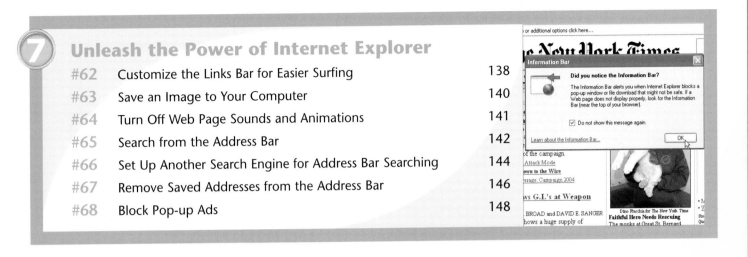
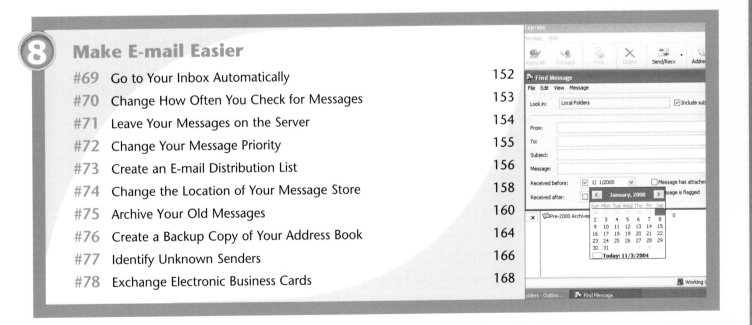

Table of Contents

Ctrl+Esc = Open S
Ctrl+Alt+Delete =

Make Windows XP Faster and More Efficient

Whether you use Windows XP at work or at home, you probably want to spend your computer time creating documents, sending and receiving e-mail, browsing the Web, playing games, and doing other useful and fun things. You probably do *not* want to spend your time wrestling with Windows XP or waiting for it to finish its tasks.

Using a few simple techniques, you can make working with Windows XP faster and more convenient. For example, rather than opening a number of Start menu folders to get to a program, you can create a shortcut in a more convenient location. If you have just set up Windows XP on a new machine, you can save yourself lots of time by transferring your old settings to the new computer.

There are also a few settings with which you can work that ensure Windows XP is working quickly and efficiently. For example, you can speed up your display by reducing the number of visual effects Windows XP uses to draw screen elements.

Sometimes getting the most out of Windows XP is a simple matter of taking care of the little things. For example, do you find yourself wasting precious time every time you accidentally press the Caps Lock key and have to delete and retype the errant text? If so, you can avoid the problem altogether by setting up Windows XP to warn you when you turn on Caps Lock.

This chapter introduces you to these and many other techniques for maximizing your Windows XP productivity.

Top 100

CREATE SHORTCUTS
for your favorite programs

If you have a program that you use regularly, you can access the program more quickly by creating a shortcut. A *shortcut* is a special file that points to a program. When you double-click the shortcut, Windows XP automatically loads that program.

Shortcuts become particularly handy when you create them in a convenient location. For example, you can create a program shortcut on your Windows XP desktop. That way, instead of clicking the Start

menu and opening a number of subfolders to find and launch a particular program, you can simply double-click the shortcut on the desktop.

You can create as many shortcuts as you want; the Windows XP desktop offers a number of features that help you keep your shortcuts organized. And if you find that you no longer use a shortcut, you can safely delete it without affecting the associated program.

This task shows you how to create and work with desktop shortcuts.

① Right-click the location on your desktop where you want to create the shortcut.

② Click New.

③ Click Shortcut.

The Create Shortcut Wizard appears.

④ Click Browse.

The Browse For Folder dialog box appears.

⑤ Select the program that you want the shortcut to start.

Note: You can also create shortcuts to documents.

⑥ Click OK.

⑦ Click Next.

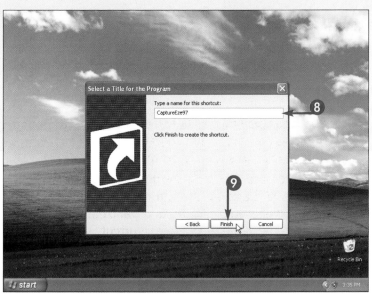

⑧ Type a name for the shortcut.

⑨ Click Finish.

● An icon for the shortcut appears.

Note: You can also customize your shortcut icons, as explained in Task #19.

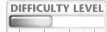

TIPS

Taskbar Trick!

The problem with adding shortcuts to your desktop is that other windows often obscure the desktop, particularly if you prefer running your program windows maximized. However, Windows gives you a quick method to get to the desktop. Right-click an empty section of the taskbar and then click Show the Desktop.

Desktop Trick!

If you frequently use the Windows XP desktop to store your program shortcuts, the desktop can quickly become a jumble of icons that make it difficult to find the shortcut you want. To solve this problem, right-click an empty spot on the desktop, click Arrange Icons By, and then Name. This sorts the shortcuts alphabetically by name.

TRANSFER YOUR SETTINGS
from an old computer

When you purchase a new computer to replace another machine, setting up the new system to use the same settings as the old one can often take a full day or more. You can save all that time for more productive pursuits by getting Windows XP to transfer those settings from your old computer and apply them automatically to your new computer. (See the following pages of this task for some examples of settings.)

You can do this by running the Files and Settings Transfer Wizard. You run this wizard in two stages. In the first stage, you run the wizard on your old computer to gather the settings. In the second stage, you run the wizard on your new computer to apply the settings.

Note, too, that the wizard can also gather files from the older computer, including the contents of your My Documents folder, your desktop, and more.

This task shows you how to use the Files and Settings Transfer Wizard.

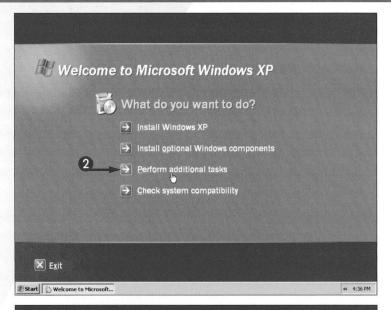

GATHER THE SETTINGS FROM YOUR OLD COMPUTER

1. If your old computer is not running Windows XP, insert the Windows XP CD on your old computer.

   Note: If your old machine runs Windows XP, click start, All Programs, Accessories, System Tools, and then Files and Settings Transfer Wizard.

   The Welcome to Microsoft Windows XP screen appears.

2. Click Perform additional tasks.

3. Click Transfer files and settings.

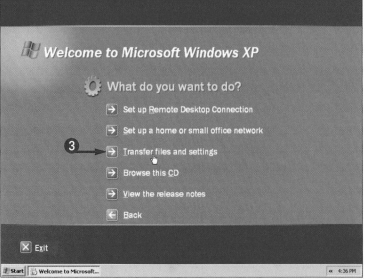

The Files and Settings
Transfer Wizard dialog
box appears.

④ Click Next.

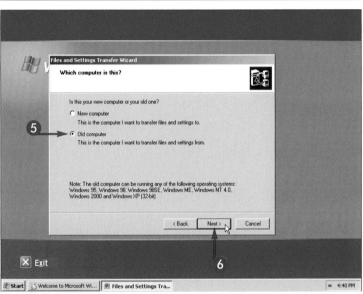

The Which computer is this? dialog box
appears.

⑤ Click Old computer (○ changes to ⊙).

⑥ Click Next.

TIPS

Attention!

If you do not have a Windows XP CD, follow
Steps **1** to **5** under the heading "Apply the
Settings to Your New Computer," later in this
task. Click "I want to create a Wizard Disk in the
following drive" (○ changes to ⊙). Insert an
empty floppy disk and click Next to create the
Wizard disk. Go to your old computer, insert
the disk, click start, and then click Run. Type
a:\fastwiz.exe and click OK to start the Files
and Settings Transfer Wizard.

Attention!

If your old computer is running Windows XP,
you can load the wizard by clicking start, All
Programs, Accessories, System Tools, and then
Files and Settings Transfer Wizard.

TRANSFER YOUR SETTINGS
from an old computer

What settings does the Files and Settings Transfer Wizard transfer? For Windows XP customization, the wizard transfers your old display settings, such as the screen colors and fonts, desktop background, screen saver, and so on; your taskbar settings; your mouse and keyboard settings; your regional settings, such as number and currency formats, country location, and installed languages; and your sound and multimedia settings.

For program settings, the wizard includes the options and data for Internet Explorer, Outlook Express, MSN Explorer, Windows Media Player, Microsoft Messenger, and Microsoft NetMeeting. The wizard also gathers

settings from certain third-party programs, including the Microsoft Office programs, Microsoft Works, Netscape, Photoshop, Quicken, RealPlayer, and others depending on what is installed on your computer.

For the files, the wizard gathers the contents of several folders, including My Documents, My Pictures, Desktop, Fonts, Shared Desktop, Shared Documents, and Quick Launch. It also gathers a long list of specific document file types, including WordPad documents, text files, all media files, as well as any file types associated with your installed third-party programs, including all Microsoft Office file types.

The Select a transfer method dialog box appears.

7 Click the transfer method that corresponds to how the two computers are connected (○ changes to ⊙).

● If you clicked Floppy drive or other removable media, click here and choose the media you want to use.

● If you clicked Other, type the name of the drive or folder in which you want to store files and settings.

8 Click Next.

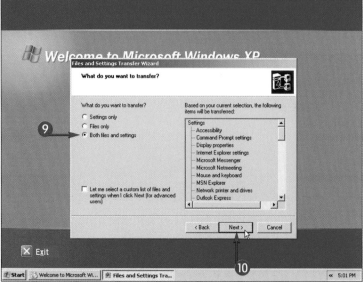

The What do you want to transfer? dialog box appears.

9 Click Both files and settings (○ changes to ⊙).

10 Click Next.

The wizard gathers your files and settings and saves them to the location or media you selected.

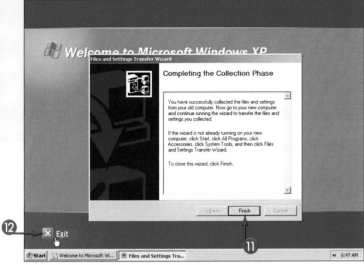

11 Click Finish.

12 Click Exit.

The Welcome to Microsoft Windows XP screen closes.

APPLY THE SETTINGS TO YOUR NEW COMPUTER

1 On the new computer, click start.

2 Click Files and Settings Transfer Wizard.

The Files and Settings Transfer Wizard appears.

Note: If you do not see the Files and Settings Transfer Wizard on the Start menu, click Start, All Programs, Accessories, System Tools, and then Files and Settings Transfer Wizard.

3 Click Next.

TIPS

Customize It!

You can create a custom list of files and settings to transfer. In the "What do you want to transfer?" dialog box, click "Let me select a custom list of files and settings" (☐ changes to ☑) and click Next. In the "Select custom files and settings" dialog box, click Add Setting, Add Folder, Add File, and Add File Type to add items to the list. To remove an item from the list, click it and then click Remove. Click Next when you have completed your custom list.

Caution!

To ensure that your files and settings are transferred properly, save any documents on which you are working and then shut down all your running programs.

TRANSFER YOUR SETTINGS
from an old computer

The Files and Settings Transfer Wizard places all the data into a single file and then compresses that file to save space. However, even basic system data will likely have at least a 10MB transfer file, and a system with lots of files and settings could easily have a transfer file that contains hundreds or thousands of megabytes.

With transfer files that big, the first transfer method you can rule out is floppy disks, which only hold about 1.44MB each. You are much better off using a DVD or CD burner, a Zip or Jaz disk, a flash drive, or some other large-capacity removable storage medium.

The next best transfer method is a direct cable connection between the two computers using a serial or parallel cable. You can use the New Connection Wizard to set this up. (Click start, All Programs, Accessories, Communications, and then New Connection Wizard.)

Finally, the best transfer method is via a network. You can save the settings to a folder, map that folder as a drive on your new computer (see Task #10), and then specify the mapped drive when you are applying the settings.

The Which computer is this dialog box appears.

4 Click New computer (○ changes to ◉).

5 Click Next.

The Do you have a Windows XP CD dialog box appears.

6 Click I don't need the Wizard Disk (○ changes to ◉).

7 Click Next.

The Where are the files and settings dialog box appears.

⑧ Click the transfer method that corresponds to how the two computers are connected (○ changes to ◉).

● If you clicked Floppy drive or other removable media, click here and choose the media you want to use.

● If you clicked Other, type the name of the drive or folder in which you want to store the files and settings.

⑨ Click Next.

The wizard applies the settings and copies the files.

The Completing the Files and Settings Transfer Wizard dialog box appears.

● This area informs you of the results of the transfer, including whether the wizard failed to transfer any of the settings.

⑩ Click Finish.

The Completing the Files and Settings Transfer Wizard dialog box closes.

Important!

If your old computer had one or more third-party programs installed, examine the list of files and settings to see if any of them refer specifically to those programs. If so, you must install those programs on your new computer before you apply the files and settings. This ensures that the third-party programs work the way they did on your old computer.

Did You Know?

If you want to know how much data the wizard will transfer, click the "Floppy drive or other removable media" option in the "Select a transfer method" dialog box (○ changes to ◉), and then click your floppy drive in the list. After you select what to transfer, the wizard determines the total amount of data and displays the total in the dialog box that prompts you to insert the first floppy disk.

ADJUST VISUAL EFFECTS
for best performance

You can turn off some or all of the visual effects that Windows XP uses to display screen elements. This reduces the load on your computer, which improves the overall performance of your machine.

These visual effects include the animation Windows XP uses when you minimize or maximize a window. For example, when you minimize a window, it appears to shrink down to the taskbar. Such effects are designed to help a novice user better understand what is happening on their computer.

For graphics in general, and the visual effects in particular, performance is mostly determined by the amount of memory on the *graphics adapter*. This is a circuit board inside your computer that processes the graphical data generated by Windows XP and displayed on your monitor. The more memory on the adapter, the faster it can process the visual effects.

Most newer computers have a decent amount of adapter memory — at least 32MB — so turning off visual effects will have little impact on performance. If your adapter has 8MB or less, turning off visual effects can improve performance.

1 Click start.

2 Right-click My Computer.

3 Click Properties.

The System Properties dialog box appears.

4 Click the Advanced tab.

5 In the Performance area, click Settings.

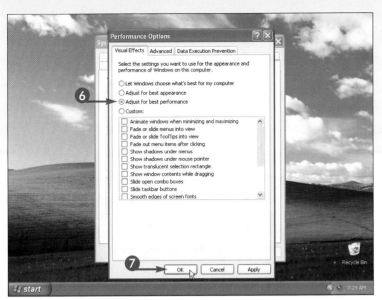

The Performance Options dialog box appears.

⑥ Click Adjust for best performance (○ changes to ⊙).

⑦ Click OK to return to the System Properties dialog box.

Windows XP turns off the visual effects.

DIFFICULTY LEVEL

⑧ Click OK.

The System Properties dialog box closes.

Customize It!

If you prefer to turn off only certain visual effects, click "Adjust for best appearance" in Step **6** (○ changes to ⊙) to ensure all the effects are activated. Click Custom (○ changes to ⊙) and then click the check box for each visual effect you want to turn off (☑ changes to ☐).

Did You Know?

If you do not know how much memory your graphics adapter has, Windows XP can tell you. Right-click the desktop and then click Properties to view the Display Properties dialog box. Click the Settings tab and then click Advanced to display the Properties dialog box for your monitor and graphics adapter. Click the Adapter tab and then read the Memory Size value in the Adapter Information area.

Ensure Windows XP is
OPTIMIZED FOR PROGRAMS

You can set some options that ensure Windows XP maximizes the performance of your programs. These options control two Windows XP tasks: processor scheduling and memory usage.

The *processor* (or *CPU*) is the chip inside your machine that coordinates all the computer's activity; some call it the "brain" of the computer. *Processor scheduling* determines how much time the processor allocates to the computer's activities. In particular, processor scheduling differentiates between the *foreground program* — the program in which you are currently working — and *background programs* — programs that perform tasks, such as printing or backing up, while you work in another program.

Memory (or *RAM*) is a set of chips inside your computer that constitute the work area of the machine. Programs and files are loaded from the hard drive into memory. Windows XP sets aside a portion of memory as the *system cache*, which holds recently used data for faster access. In terms of *memory usage*, the bigger the system cache, the less memory is available for your programs, which can reduce performance.

This task shows you how to set the processor scheduling and memory usage to optimize program performance.

① Click start.

② Right-click My Computer.

③ Click Properties.

The System Properties dialog box appears.

④ Click the Advanced tab.

⑤ In the Performance area, click Settings.

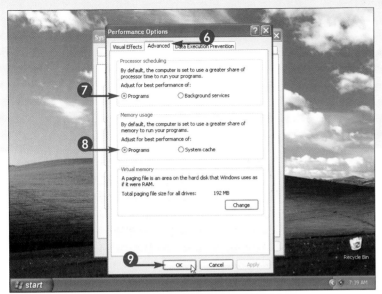

The Performance Options dialog box appears.

6 Click the Advanced tab.

7 In the Processor scheduling area, click Programs (○ changes to ⊙).

8 In the Memory usage area, click Programs (○ changes to ⊙).

9 Click OK to return to the System Properties dialog box.

Windows XP applies the performance settings.

10 Click OK.

The System Properties dialog box closes.

Note: You can also increase the performance of individual programs, as explained in Task #5.

4

DIFFICULTY LEVEL

TIPS

Did You Know?
There are circumstances where you may be better off clicking the System cache option (○ changes to ⊙) in the Advanced tab of the Performance Options dialog box. Specifically, any programs that are extremely data-intensive can benefit from a larger system cache. Such programs include high-end graphics software, video-editing software, and databases that deal with large files.

Did You Know?
If you do not know what kind of processor or how much memory your computer has, Windows XP can tell you. Click start, right-click My Computer, and then click Properties to view the System Properties dialog box. Click the General tab and then read the information in the Computer area.

ADJUST A PROGRAM'S PRIORITY
for better performance

You can improve the performance of a program by adjusting the priority given to the program by your computer's processor.

The processor enables programs to run by doling out thin slivers of its computing time to each program. These time slivers are called *cycles* because they are given to programs cyclically. For example, if you have three programs running — A, B, and C — the processor gives a cycle to A, one to B, another to C, and then back to A again. This cycling happens quickly, appearing seamless when you work with each program.

The *base priority* is a ranking that determines the relative frequency with which a program gets processor cycles. A program given a higher priority gets more cycles, which improves the program's performance. For example, suppose you raise the priority of program A. The processor may give a cycle to A, one to B, another to A, one to C, another to A, and so on.

This task shows you how to adjust the base priority for a given program.

① Right-click an empty section of the taskbar.

② Click Task Manager.

The Task Manager window appears.

③ Click the Processes tab.

This list shows all the processes currently running on your computer.

Note: A process is anything that requires processor time. This includes not only your running programs, but also the services and programs that Windows XP itself uses to perform housekeeping and other chores.

④ Right-click the program with which you want to work.

⑤ Click Set Priority.

⑥ Click the priority level you want to apply to the program.

Windows XP adjusts the program's priority.

In this example, WordPad's priority is increased to AboveNormal so that Windows can give the program more processing cycles.

⑦ Click here to close the Task Manager window.

TIPS

Customize It!

After you change the priority of one or more programs, you may forget the values that you have assigned to each one. To help, you can view the priority for all the items in the Processes tab. Click View and then click Select Columns to display the Select Columns dialog box. Click Base Priority (☐ changes to ☑) and click OK. This adds a Base Priority column to the Processes list.

Did You Know?

If you are not sure which process is associated with the program you want to work with, click the Task Manager's Applications tab. This tab displays a list of your running programs. Right-click the program with which you want to work and then click Go To Process. Windows XP switches to the Processes tab and selects the program's process in the list.

TURN OFF CONFIRMATION
for deleted files

DIFFICULTY LEVEL

You can save a step each time you delete a file by turning off the Recycle Bin's confirmation dialog box.

Each time you delete a file in Windows XP, the Confirm File Delete dialog box appears, asking if you are sure you want to send the file to the Recycle Bin. If you find this extra step unnecessary or inefficient, you can adjust the Recycle Bin's properties to turn off the confirmation prompt.

More Options!

If you do not want to use the Recycle Bin at all, Windows XP offers two methods for deleting a file immediately. If you prefer to delete a file immediately only occasionally, click the file and then press the Shift+Delete keys. To delete all files immediately, follow Steps **1** and **2** to display the Recycle Bin Properties dialog box, click the "Do not move files to the Recycle Bin" option (☐ changes to ☑), and then click OK.

① Right-click the desktop's Recycle Bin icon.

② Click Properties.

The Recycle Bin Properties dialog box appears.

③ Click Display delete confirmation dialog (☑ changes to ☐).

④ Click OK.

When you delete a file from now on, Windows XP will not ask you to confirm.

HEAR AN ALERT
when you press the Caps Lock key

DIFFICULTY LEVEL

TIP

You can adjust a setting that tells Windows XP to beep your computer's speaker whenever you press the Caps Lock key. This can be a real timesaver when you press Caps Lock by accident. As you probably know, when you inadvertently press Caps Lock, it may be a while before you realize it, and you end up with a great deal of typing that has the capital letters reversed. Not only must you delete this text, but you must also retype it with the correct letters. Hearing an alert when you press Caps Lock means you can avoid this extra work.

Did You Know?

You can also activate the ToggleKeys setting by holding down the Num Lock key for five seconds. You hear a beep and the ToggleKeys dialog box appears. Click OK to keep ToggleKeys turned on; click Cancel to turn ToggleKeys off. If you want to disable the Num Lock shortcut, click Settings to display the Keyboard tab of the Accessibility Options dialog box, click Settings in the ToggleKeys area, click Use Shortcut (☑ changes to ☐), and then click OK.

① Click start.

② Click Control Panel.

The Control Panel window appears.

③ Click Accessibility Options.

④ In the Accessibility Options window, click Accessibility Options.

⑤ In the Accessibility Options dialog box, click the Keyboard tab.

⑥ Click Use ToggleKeys (☐ changes to ☑).

⑦ Click OK.

⑧ Click here to close the Accessibility Options window.

Windows will alert you with a tone when you press the Caps Lock key.

Force Windows XP to
USE LESS DISK SPACE

You can adjust the settings of three different Windows XP components to force those components to use less hard drive space.

Although most of today's hard drives are quite large, it is still possible for hard drive space to become scarce. When this happens, many people try to resolve the problem by deleting a few files or uninstalling a program. Unfortunately, in most cases these remedies only save a few megabytes. With the techniques you learn in this task, you can easily save hundreds or even thousands of megabytes.

The three components you work with in this task are the Recycle Bin, System Restore, and Internet Explorer. You learn about the latter two components later in this task.

The Recycle Bin uses disk space to store deleted files temporarily. However, Windows XP sets aside 10 percent of the hard drive to store these files. On a 20GB hard drive, this represents 2GB. Reducing the Recycle Bin usage to 5 percent saves you 1GB.

REDUCE RECYCLE BIN DISK USAGE

① Right-click the desktop's Recycle Bin icon.

② Click Properties.

The Recycle Bin Properties dialog box appears.

● The slider determines the percentage of hard drive space allocated to the Recycle Bin files.

③ Click and drag the slider to the left to reduce the percentage.

④ Click OK.

Windows now uses less space for the Recycle Bin.

① Click start.

② Right-click My Computer.

③ Click Properties.

DIFFICULTY LEVEL

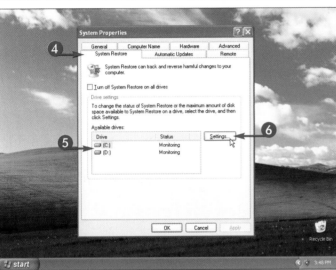

The System Properties dialog box appears.

④ Click the System Restore tab.

⑤ Click the drive with which you want to work.

⑥ Click Settings.

More Options!

You can also reclaim hard drive space using the Disk Cleanup program. Click start, All Programs, Accessories, System Tools, and then Disk Cleanup.

Caution!

You can save even more hard drive space by reducing to a minimum the percentage used by the Recycle Bin. However, this is dangerous because it also compromises the effectiveness of this tool. Minimizing the Recycle Bin's disk space usage means that deleted files will be stored only for a short time, so you may not be able to recover an accidentally deleted file.

Force Windows XP to
USE LESS DISK SPACE

The other two Windows XP components that you modify in this task are System Restore and Internet Explorer.

System Restore uses hard drive space to save its restore points, which are "snapshots" of your system state. You can use these restore points to restore your malfunctioning system to an earlier, working configuration. By default, the program takes up 12 percent of the hard drive for this purpose, which is usually enough to store several weeks' worth of restore points. If you halve this percentage, you still

save enough restore points and you reclaim 1.2GB on a 20GB hard drive.

Internet Explorer uses hard drive space to store its temporary Internet files, which are local copies of Web site files that the program uses to make sites display faster the next time you access them. The amount of disk space used depends on the size of the hard drive and the amount of free space, but you can generally save a few hundred megabytes by reducing the disk space usage.

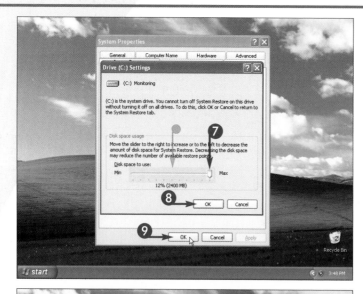

The drive's Settings dialog box appears.

● The slider determines the percentage of hard drive space used for the restore points created by System Restore.

⑦ Click and drag the slider to the left to reduce the percentage.

⑧ Click OK to return to the System Properties dialog box.

⑨ Click OK.

Windows now uses less System Restore disk space.

REDUCE INTERNET EXPLORER DISK USAGE

① Click start.

② Right-click Internet.

③ Click Internet Properties.

Note: If your Start menu's Internet icon launches a browser other than Internet Explorer, click start, Control Panel, Network, Internet Connections, and then Internet Options.

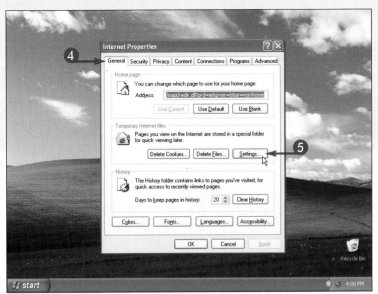

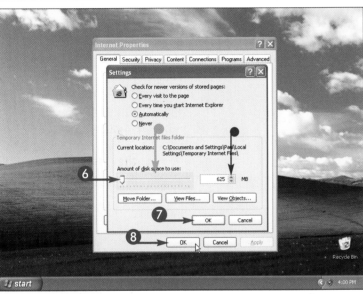

The Internet Properties dialog box appears.

④ Click the General tab.

⑤ Click Settings.

The Settings dialog box appears.

● The slider determines the percentage of hard disk space used for the temporary Internet files.

⑥ Click and drag the slider to the left to reduce the percentage.

● You can also click here to set the amount of disk space, in megabytes.

⑦ Click OK to return to the Internet Properties dialog box.

⑧ Click OK.

Windows now uses less space for Internet Explorer.

TIPS

Caution!

Avoid reducing to a minimum the percentage used by System Restore and Internet Explorer because this minimizes the usefulness of these programs. For example, minimizing System Restore's disk space usage sharply reduces the number of saved restore points. This may prevent you from restoring your computer to a previously working state. Similarly, minimizing the number of saved temporary Internet files can slow down your Web surfing.

More Options!

If your hard drive uses NTFS (New Technology File System), you can save even more disk space by compressing the drive. In My Computer, click the hard drive, click File, and then click Properties to open the drive's Properties dialog box. Click the "Compress drive to save disk space" option (☐ changes to ☑).

Disable
FAST USER SWITCHING

You can speed up the performance of your computer by turning off Windows XP's Fast User Switching feature.

Windows XP supports *user accounts* that enable different people to log on and use the system with their own settings for the desktop, display, Start menu, taskbar, Internet Explorer favorites, Outlook Express accounts, and their own documents.

The *Fast User Switching* feature enables a second person to log on to his or her account while the first person's programs and documents remain open but temporarily hidden from view. (To try this out, click start, Log Off, Switch User, and then the name of the user who wants to log on.)

This is a convenient feature, but it comes at a price: the original user's open programs and documents remain in memory, which reduces the overall memory available for the second user. And because Windows XP enables multiple users to be logged on at the same time, each set of open programs and documents reduces the memory available for all the users. In general, the less memory available, the slower your computer will run.

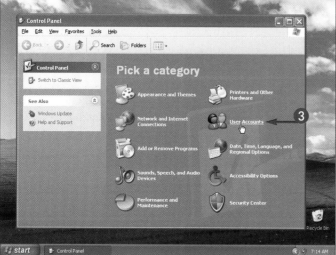

① Click start.

② Click Control Panel.

The Control Panel window appears.

③ Click User Accounts.

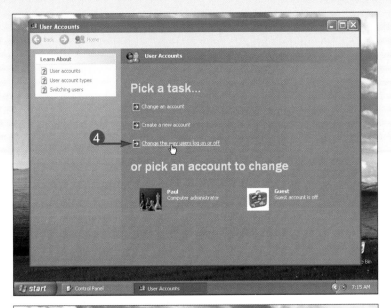

The User Accounts window appears.

④ Click Change the way users log on or off.

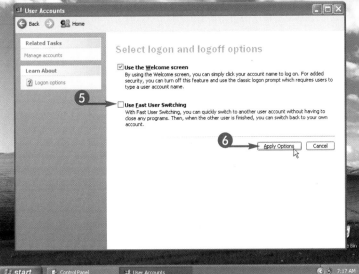

The Select logon and logoff options window appears.

⑤ Click Use Fast User Switching (☑ changes to ☐).

⑥ Click Apply Options.

Windows disables Fast User Switching.

Note: See Task #79 to learn how to protect your user account with a password.

TIPS

Did You Know?

The reduction in performance caused by Fast User Switching only occurs on computers that have a small amount of memory: say, 128MB of RAM or less. If you want the convenience of this feature, then you must add more memory to your system. Ideally, you should add at least another 64MB for each user. (See Task #4 to find out how much memory is installed on your computer.)

Try This!

Another advantage you gain by disabling Fast User Switching is the ability to quickly lock your computer so that no one else can use it or view what is on your screen if your username is password protected. Press the Windows Logo+L keys. Windows XP clears the screen and displays the Unlock Computer dialog box, which prompts for your account password.

DISPLAY A NETWORK FOLDER
as a disk drive on your computer

You can gain easier access to a shared network folder by displaying the folder as though it was a disk drive on your computer.

If your computer is part of a network, you can use My Network Places to view the folders that other users have shared on the network. This is convenient most of the time, but there are two circumstances where it is not. First, if you want to work with a subfolder, you must open the shared folder and then drill down through the subfolders until you get the one you want. Second, if the folder does not appear

in My Network Places, you must open your workgroup, open the computer that contains the folder, and then open the folder.

Both of these scenarios are inefficient and time consuming, particularly if you access the contents of the folder regularly. To save time, Windows XP enables you to display any shared network folder as though it were a disk drive on your computer. This is called *mapping* the network folder. The advantage of mapping is that an icon for the mapped folder appears in My Computer, so you can simply double-click the icon to access the folder.

1 Click start.

2 Click My Network Places.

Note: If you do not see the My Network Places icon on the Start menu, click My Computer and then My Network Places.

The My Network Places window appears.

3 Click Tools.

4 Click Map Network Drive.

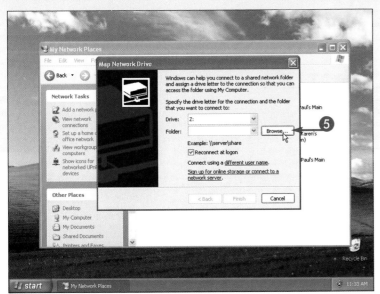

The Map Network Drive dialog box appears.

⑤ Click Browse.

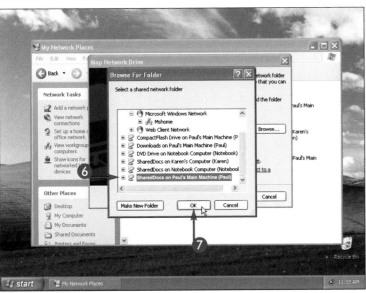

The Browse For Folder dialog box appears.

⑥ Click the shared network folder with which you want to work.

⑦ Click OK to return to the Map Network Drive dialog box.

More Options!

Here is a faster way to open the Map Network Drive dialog box: Click start, right-click My Computer or My Network Places, and then click Map Network Drive.

Customize It!

If you think you will be mapping a different network folder frequently, you can add a Map Drive button to the My Computer toolbar. Click View, Toolbars, and then Customize to display the Customize Toolbar dialog box. In the Available toolbar buttons list, click Map Drive and then click Add. Click Close. The Map Drive button (▣) appears on your My Computer toolbar.

DISPLAY A NETWORK FOLDER
as a disk drive on your computer

Another advantage that comes with mapping network folders to local disk drive letters is that it can solve problems that occur with certain programs.

Some software programs — particularly older Windows programs and MS-DOS programs — are programmed to work only with local files, meaning that they cannot handle shared network folders directly. You can work around this problem by mapping a drive letter to the shared network folder. This makes it appear as though the network folder is part of your local computer, which is almost always enough to fool these older programs.

Given all these advantages of mapped network folders, you may decide to use them often. Remember, however, that you are limited by the number of available drive letters on your computer. For example, suppose your computer has a floppy disk drive (drive A), two hard disk drives (drives C and D), a CD-ROM drive (drive E), and a DVD-ROM drive (drive F). This leaves 21 available drive letters: B and G through Z.

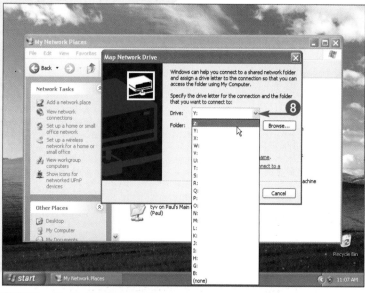

⑧ Click here and then click the drive letter you want to assign to the network folder.

● If you do not want Windows XP to assign the drive letter to the network folder each time you start your computer, you can click Reconnect at Logon (☑ changes to ☐).

⑨ Click Finish.

A window showing the contents of the network folder appears.

⑩ Click My Computer.

The My Computer window appears.

● An icon for the drive letter appears in My Computer's Network Drives section.

TIPS

Caution!

If you use a removable drive such as CompactFlash memory module, Windows XP automatically assigns a drive letter to such a drive. This often causes a conflict if you have a mapped network folder that uses a lower drive letter (such as D, E, or F). Therefore, using higher drive letters (such as X, Y, and Z) for your mapped network folders is good practice.

Remove It!

To speed up the Windows XP startup and reduce clutter in My Computer, you can disconnect mapped network folders that you no longer use. To disconnect a mapped folder, click start and then My Computer. In the Network Drives section, right-click the network drive you want to disconnect and then click Disconnect.

2

Set Up Windows XP the Way You Want

Windows XP is endlessly customizable and offers many features that enable you to modify the look and feel of your system to suit your style and the way you work.

You probably already know how to customize aspects of the Windows XP screen such as the colors, fonts, desktop background, and screen resolution. These are useful techniques to know, to be sure, but Windows XP offers a number of other techniques that put much more emphasis on what is practical. That is, although changing your screen colors might make Windows XP more interesting, it does not help you get your work done any faster. However, a technique such as revamping your Start menu for easy access to your most-used programs can save you lots of mouse clicks and, ultimately, lots of time.

This chapter focuses on the practical aspects of customizing Windows XP by showing you a number of techniques, most of which are designed to save you time and make Windows XP more efficient. You begin with several techniques that make your Start menu much easier to deal with, including adding icons permanently, removing unneeded icons, increasing the number of programs, and displaying the Control Panel as an easy-to-access menu.

Other techniques in this chapter include creating a custom program access configuration for your Web browser, e-mail program, and more; scheduling Windows XP to automatically download program updates; and synchronizing your system time with an Internet time server. You also learn how to customize your desktop and shortcut icons.

Top 100

PIN AN ITEM
to your Start menu

You can customize the Windows XP Start menu to give yourself quick access to the programs that you use most often.

The items on the main Start menu — including My Computer and the Internet and E-mail icons — are very handy because they require just two clicks to launch. To start up all your other programs, you must also click All Programs and then negotiate one or more submenus. For those programs you use most often, you can avoid this extra work by *pinning* their icons permanently to the main Start menu, the process of which is demonstrated in this task.

Reverse It!
All pinned program items appear on the left side of the Start menu, in the top section where the Internet and E-mail icons reside. If you have pinned several programs and you find this section is getting too crowded, you can remove a pinned item by right-clicking the item and then clicking Unpin from Start menu.

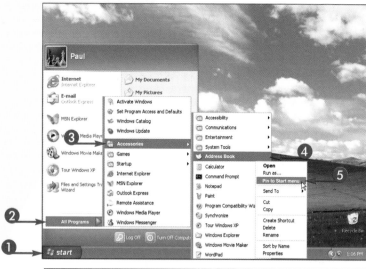

① Click start.

② Click All Programs.

③ Open the submenu that contains the program you want to pin to the Start menu.

④ Right-click the program icon.

⑤ Click Pin to Start menu.

● Windows XP adds the program to the main Start menu.

● You can also pin any of the often-used program items to the main Start menu.

REMOVE AN ITEM
from your Start menu

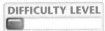

You can remove Start menu program items that you no longer use, reducing the clutter and allowing other often-used programs to appear.

The left side of the main Start menu is divided into two sections. The top part consists of menu items that remain in place, including the Internet and E-mail icons and any "pinned" program items. The bottom part consists of the six programs that you have used most often, so these change as you use your computer. You can remove programs that you no longer use from either section on the left side of the Start menu.

More Options!
You can also delete items — including not only program items but also entire submenus — from the All Programs menu and its various submenus. To do this, click start, All Programs, and then open the menu that contains the item you want to delete. Right-click the item and then click Delete. When Windows XP asks you to confirm the deletion, click Yes.

❶ Click start.

❷ Right-click the item you want to remove.

❸ Click Remove from This List.

● Windows XP removes the item from the Start menu.

Note: *See also Task #13 to learn how to show more programs on the Start menu.*

CHANGE THE NUMBER OF PROGRAMS
on your Start menu

You can customize the Start menu to display more or fewer of the programs you use most often.

The list displaying your most-frequently used programs appears on the bottom-left side of the Start menu, above All Programs. As you work with your programs, Windows XP keeps track of how many times you launch each one. The programs that you have launched most often appear on the Start menu for easy, two-click access. These programs appear at the top of the list, followed by the next

most-often-used programs, and so on. When another program becomes popular, Windows XP drops the bottom program and adds the new one.

Unfortunately, the default Start menu shows just the six most popular programs. If you find that some of your regular programs are constantly getting dropped from the Start menu, you can increase the size of the list to force Windows XP to display more programs.

① Right-click start.

② Click Properties.

The Taskbar and Start Menu Properties dialog box appears.

③ Click the Start Menu tab.

④ Click Customize.

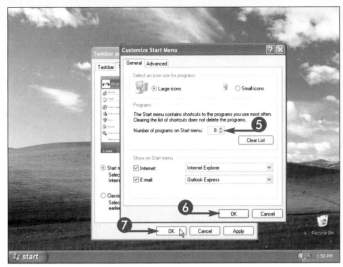

The Customize Start Menu dialog box appears.

⑤ Enter the number of programs you want to see.

Note: The maximum number of programs is 30.

DIFFICULTY LEVEL

⑥ Click OK to return to the Taskbar and Start Menu Properties dialog box.

⑦ Click OK.

● Windows XP adjusts the size of the Start menu's most-frequently used program list.

TIPS

More Options!

You may find that Windows XP displays fewer items in the list of frequently used programs than you have specified. That happens because the height of the Start menu — and the number of items in the program list — is restricted by the height of your screen. To display more items without changing the screen height, follow Steps **1** to **4** to open the Customize Start Menu dialog box. Click Small icons (○ changes to ◉), and then click OK. Using smaller icons enables more items to appear on the Start menu.

Customize It!

If you want to get even more items on the Start menu, you can change the height of your screen by increasing the screen resolution. Right-click the desktop, click Properties, and then click the Settings tab in the Display Properties dialog box. Click and drag the Screen Resolution slider to the left, and then click OK.

SHOW CONTROL PANEL
as a menu on your Start menu

You can quickly access items in the Control Panel by converting the Start menu's Control Panel item into a menu.

Control Panel is Windows XP's customization shop, with well over two-dozen icons. Using these icons, you can customize and modify features such as accessibility, the display, folders and fonts, the Internet, and user accounts. You can install and uninstall programs and devices, and you can tweak specific devices such as game controllers, the keyboard, the mouse, the modem, printers, scanners, and more.

The longer you use Windows XP, the more you appreciate the Control Panel. The problem, however, is that the default Control Panel window uses a Category View that groups the Control Panel icons into categories such as Appearance and Themes and Printers and Other Hardware. That view hampers more experienced users, who must often negotiate several windows to get to the icon they want. Converting the Start menu's Control Panel item into a menu on the Start menu enables you to easily find and choose any Control Panel item.

① Right-click start.

② Click Properties.

The Taskbar and Start Menu Properties dialog box appears.

③ Click the Start Menu tab.

④ Click Customize.

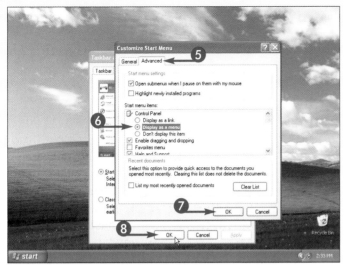

The Customize Start Menu dialog box appears.

⑤ Click the Advanced tab.

⑥ In the Start menu items list, under Control Panel, click Display as a menu (○ changes to ⊙).

⑦ Click OK to return to the Taskbar and Start Menu Properties dialog box.

⑧ Click OK.

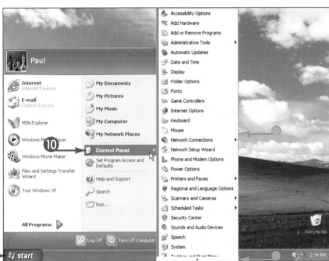

⑨ Click start.

⑩ Click Control Panel.

● A menu of the Control Panel items appears.

● If the entire menu does not fit on your screen, position the mouse here to expand the menu.

TIPS

More Options!

There are other Start menu items that you can display as menus. Follow Steps **1** to **5** to display the Advanced tab of the Customize Start Menu dialog box. The following branches have a "Display as a menu" option that you can click (○ changes to ⊙): My Computer, My Documents, My Pictures, and My Music.

More Options!

For easier access to some of your documents, follow Steps **1** to **5** to display the Advanced tab of the Customize Start Menu dialog box. Click Favorites menu (☐ changes to ☑) to display a menu of Internet Explorer favorites. Also, you can click "List my most recently opened documents" (☐ changes to ☑) to display a list of the 15 documents you have used most recently.

Create a custom
PROGRAM ACCESS CONFIGURATION

You can modify Windows XP to use other programs as the default for activities such as Web browsing, e-mail, instant messaging, and media playing. This enables you to have your favorite programs available in more convenient locations, and to have those programs launch automatically in certain situations.

Your version of Windows XP is most likely set up to use Internet Explorer, Outlook Express, Windows Messenger, and Windows Media Player as the default programs for Web browsing, e-mail, instant messaging, and media playing, respectively. This

means that Internet Explorer and Outlook Express are associated with the Start menu's Internet and E-mail items. Also, it means these programs launch automatically in response to certain events. For example, an audio CD you insert plays in Windows Media Player.

You can set up as defaults any other programs you may have installed for Web browsing, e-mail, instant messaging, and media playing. You can also disable access to programs so that other users cannot launch them on your computer.

❶ Click start.

❷ Click Set Program Access and Defaults.

The Add or Remove Programs window appears with the Set Program Access and Defaults screen in view.

❸ Click Custom (○ changes to ⊙).

❹ Click here to view more information about the configuration.

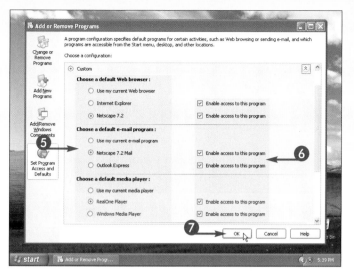

The Set Program Access and Defaults options appear.

⑤ Click the program you prefer to use for Web browsing, e-mailing, and playing media.

⑥ For each listed program, if you want to disable access, click Enable access to this program (☑ changes to ☐).

⑦ Click OK.

⑧ Click start.

● The Internet and E-mail items reflect your browser and e-mail program choices in Step **5**.

Important!

To use the Set Program Access and Defaults tool, you must be logged on to Windows XP with administrator privileges. Also, this tool was not available in the original release of Windows XP. You must install Service Pack 1 or later to have access to the Set Program Access and Defaults tool.

More Options!

If you just want to change the programs associated with the Start menu's Internet and E-mail items, follow Steps **1** to **4** in Task #13 to open the Customize Start Menu dialog box. Click ☑ in the Internet and E-mail lists and then click the programs you prefer.

Schedule
AUTOMATIC UPDATES

You can configure Windows XP's Automatic Updates feature to automatically check for, download, and install available updates. By choosing a time that is convenient for you, you ensure that your computer always has the most up-to-date features of Windows XP.

Windows XP is a work in progress; the programmers are constantly finding and fixing small errors in Windows XP. More importantly, however, the world — particularly the online world — is becoming ever more dangerous. System intruders are a constant threat, and viruses, worms, and other malevolent

programs multiply by the hour. To thwart these and other malicious elements, the Windows XP team regularly issues "patches" and updates that plug security leaks and beef up XP's protection features.

However, you likely do not have the time or patience to track down and install all these updates yourself. Fortunately, you do not have to because Windows XP comes with a handy Automatic Updates feature. As shown in this task, you can set up Automatic Updates to automatically download and install the latest updates at a time that works best for you.

① Click the Security Center icon in the taskbar's notification area.

The Windows Security Center window appears.

② Click Automatic Updates.

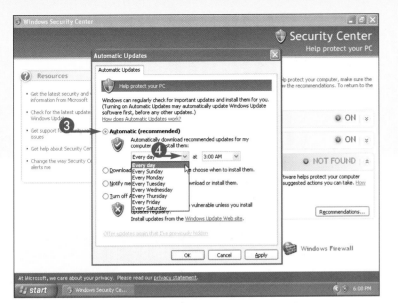

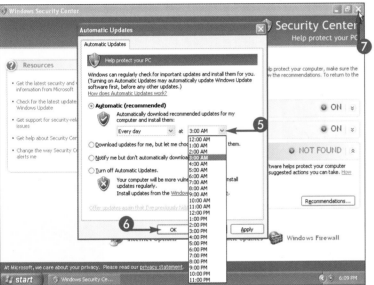

The Automatic Updates dialog box appears.

#16

DIFFICULTY LEVEL

③ Click Automatic (○ changes to ⊙).

④ Click here and then click the day on which you want Windows XP to check for updates.

⑤ Click here and then click the time at which you want Windows XP to check for updates.

⑥ Click OK.

⑦ Click here to shut down the Windows Security Center window.

Windows will automatically check for updates at the day and time you specified.

Important!

The automatic update only occurs if your computer is turned on and connected to the Internet. If your computer is off or offline when the update is scheduled to occur, Automatic Updates runs the update the next time you connect to the Internet. If you do not want the update to occur while you are using your computer, schedule it for a time when you will be away from the computer but still connected to the Internet.

More Options!

If you prefer to take control of the updates, follow Steps **1** to **2** to display the Automatic Updates dialog box. Click "Notify me but don't automatically download or install them" (○ changes to ⊙) and then click OK.

SYNCHRONIZE
your system time

You can keep your system time accurate by synchronizing the time with a server computer on the Internet.

Your computer has an internal clock that keeps track of the current date and time. Windows XP displays the clock's current time in the taskbar, to the right of the notification area. To view the current date, position the mouse over the time until the date appears. For many people, the Windows XP clock has replaced the traditional wall or desktop clock in the office or den.

Unfortunately, computer clocks are not always very accurate. It is not unusual for the system clock to gain or lose a minute or two a day. Clearly, if you are relying on the Windows XP clock to know what time it is, you want the clock to be accurate.

Windows XP can help by enabling you to synchronize the clock with an accurate source. The Internet offers a number of computers called *time servers* that maintain the accurate time. Windows XP can synchronize with a time server to keep your system clock correct.

❶ Connect to the Internet.

❷ Click start.

❸ Click Control Panel.

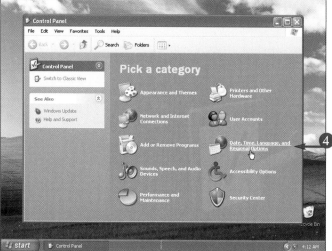

The Control Panel window appears.

❹ Click Date, Time, Language, and Regional Options.

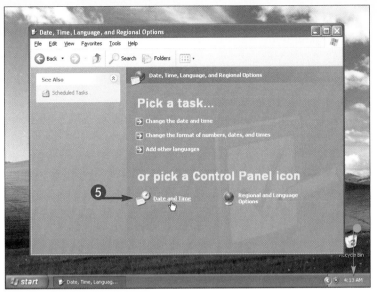

The Date, Time, Language, and Regional Options window appears.

5 Click Date and Time.

● You can also display the Date and Time Properties dialog box by double-clicking the time display in the taskbar.

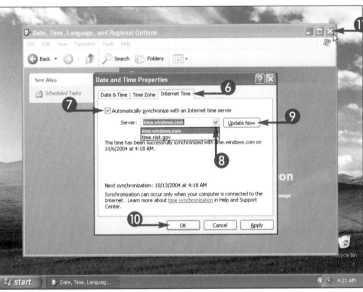

6 In the Date and Time Properties dialog box, click the Internet Time tab.

7 Click Automatically synchronize with an Internet time server (□ changes to ☑).

8 Click here and then click the time server you want to use.

9 Click Update Now.

Windows XP synchronizes your system time.

10 Click OK.

11 Click here to close the window.

Check It Out!

The two default time servers — time.windows.com and time.nist.gov — are usually reliable and accurate. You can also type another time server's address in the Server text box. Here are two sites that maintain lists of time server addresses: www.boulder.nist.gov/timefreq/service/time-servers.html
http://ntp.isc.org/bin/view/Servers/NTPPoolServers

Troubleshoot It!

If you are unable to synchronize your system time, first make sure you are connected to the Internet. Also, check that your computer's time and date are not wildly off the current date and time — say, by a day or more. If they are, click the Date & Time tab in the Date and Time Properties dialog box and set a time and date that are close to the current values. Finally, check that your Internet firewall software allows time synchronization.

Customize your
DESKTOP ICONS

You can make your desktop more useful by adding some standard Windows XP icons, such as My Computer and My Documents. You can also customize those icons to display a different image.

The collection of icons on the Windows XP desktop depends on a number of factors: whether you upgraded from an earlier version of Windows, in which case your old icons will have been preserved; whether the manufacturer of your computer customized the desktop; and whether the third-party programs you have installed have added their own

icons to the desktop. In most cases, however, the Windows XP desktop contains but a single icon: the Recycle Bin.

If you are looking to make your desktop more useful, Windows XP offers a couple of methods to do just that. For one, you can add shortcuts for your favorite programs to the desktop, as shown in Task #1. For another, you can add shortcuts for four common Windows XP features: My Computer, My Documents, My Network Places, and Internet Explorer; you learn how this is done in this task. You also learn how to customize those icons with different images.

① Right-click the desktop.

② Click Properties.

The Display Properties dialog box appears.

③ Click the Desktop tab.

④ Click Customize Desktop.

The Desktop Items dialog box appears.

⑤ Click the check box for each icon you want to add to the desktop (☐ changes to ☑).

⑥ Click the icon you want to customize.

⑦ Click Change Icon.

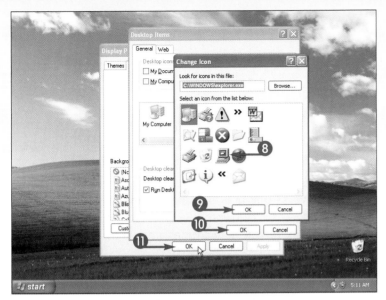

The Change Icon dialog box appears.

⑧ Click the icon you want to use.

⑨ Click OK to return to the Desktop Items dialog box.

⑩ Click OK to return to the Display Properties dialog box.

⑪ Click OK.

 # 18

DIFFICULTY LEVEL

● The new icon with the appearance you chose appears on the desktop.

TIPS

More Options!

The icons shown in the Change Icon dialog box are not the only ones available. By changing the filename in the text box, you can display a new set of icons from which you can choose. Here are some files to try (replace C:\Windows with the location of your Windows files, if necessary):
C:\Windows\system32\shell32.dll
C:\Windows\system32\moricons.dll
C:\Windows\system32\pifmgr.dll

Check It Out!

If you feel creative, you can make your own icons using an icon editor program such as Microangelo, IconCool, or IconForge. These and other icon editors are available from www.download.com.

Make your desktop icons
EASIER TO SEE

You can make your desktop icons easier to see and read by making them larger and by increasing their contrast with the desktop background.

Most of today's computers have monitors and graphics adapters capable of running at high screen resolutions. This gives you much more room to display windows and other items, but there is a cost: the higher the screen resolution, the smaller all the screen elements appear. You may have difficulty seeing your desktop icons and reading the tiny icon text, particularly when your desktop uses a busy

background image such as the default Bliss wallpaper. And certainly you have double the problem if your eyesight is not what it used to be.

Fortunately, Windows XP enables you to fix this by giving you control over the size of the desktop icons as well as the font used for the icon text. By increasing the size of the icons, increasing the size of the icon font, and making the font bold for contrast with the desktop, you can make your icons much easier to see and read.

① Right-click the desktop.

② Click Properties.

The Display Properties dialog box appears.

③ Click the Appearance tab.

④ Click Advanced.

The Advanced Appearance dialog box appears.

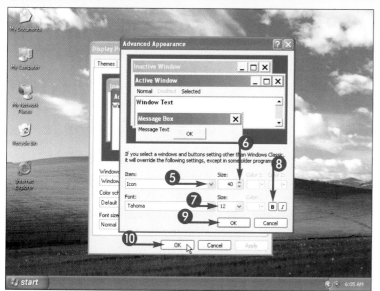

⑤ Click here and then click Icon.

⑥ Click the Size box and type a larger icon size.

⑦ To increase the font size, click the Size box and type the new size.

⑧ Click here to bold the icon text for easier reading.

⑨ Click OK to return to the Display Properties dialog box.

⑩ Click OK.

DIFFICULTY LEVEL

● Windows XP applies the changes to the desktop icons.

TIPS

Desktop Trick!
Another feature that can make desktop icons difficult to read is the drop shadow that Windows XP applies to the icon text. To remove the drop shadow, follow Steps **1** to **5** in Task #3 to display the Performance Options dialog box. Click Custom (○ changes to ⊙) and then click "Use drop shadows for icon labels on the desktop" (☑ changes to ☐). Click OK.

More Options!
For the best contrast between the desktop background and the desktop icon labels, use a solid color background, and then choose a color for the icon text that contrasts sharply with the color you chose. In general, light-colored text on a dark-colored background is easiest to read.

Chapter 2: Set Up Windows XP the Way You Want   47

Chapter 3

Enrich Your Media Experience

Windows XP was designed from the ground up to offer you a rich media experience. Whether you are dealing with drawings, photos, sounds, audio CDs, downloaded music files, or DVDs, the tools that are built into Windows XP enable you to play, edit, and even create media.

The downside to having a rich media environment at your fingertips is that the media tools themselves are necessarily feature-laden and complex. The basic operations are usually easy enough to master, but some of the more useful and interesting features tend to be in hard-to-find places. This chapter helps you take advantage of many of these off-the-beaten-track features by showing you how to find and use them.

For example, you will learn lots of useful image tips and tricks, including how to convert any folder into a powerful media folder; how to publish your images to a Web site; how to load images into a graphics program with a double-click; how to compress images so they take up less space; and how to annotate an image with your own comments and notes.

On the audio front, you learn how to associate sounds with certain Windows XP events such as maximizing and minimizing a window and opening a program. For Windows Media Player, you learn how to activate the handy Mini Player toolbar; how to modify the audio and video playback settings; how to disable the recording of CDs; and how to set parental controls for watching DVDs.

Top 100

Customize a media folder by
APPLYING A TEMPLATE

You can customize a folder according to the type of media it contains, giving you easier access to some of the Windows XP features related to that type of media.

Windows XP is designed to make certain features and tasks available only when it makes sense. This means that the interface changes depending on what type of file, folder, or other object with which you are working. For example, consider the taskbar, which appears on the left side of any folder window. The

taskbar displays a collection of links that run tasks related to the folder or to any selected file within the folder.

For example, when you open the My Pictures folder, the taskbar includes items such as View as Slide Show and Print Pictures; similarly, if you select a music file in the My Music folder, the taskbar includes Play Selection and Copy to Audio CD.

You can access this very useful feature in any of your folders by applying the appropriate folder template, as described in this task.

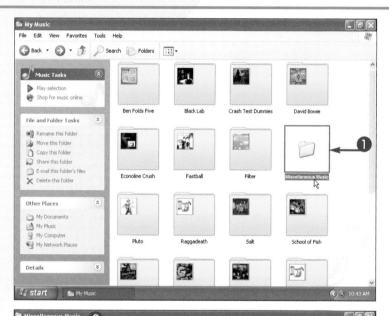

① Double-click the folder you want to customize.

The folder's content appears.

② Click View.

③ Click Customize This Folder.

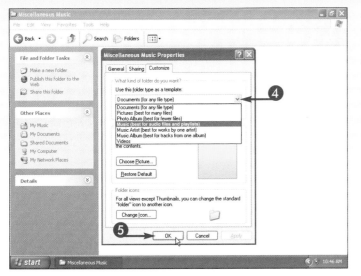

The folder's Properties dialog box appears.

④ Click here and then click the template you want to apply to the folder.

⑤ Click OK.

DIFFICULTY LEVEL

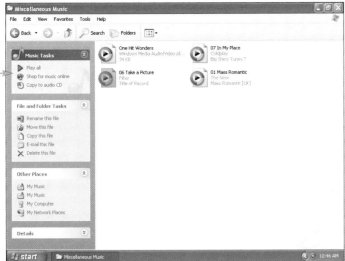

Windows XP applies the template to the folder.

● This area now shows tasks related to the type of folder template you selected.

More Options!

If you have subfolders that contain similar files, you do not have to open each folder and apply the template. Instead, follow Steps **1** to **4** to select a template for the main folder, and then click the "Also apply this template to all subfolders" option (☐ changes to ☑).

Customize It!

To remind yourself of the template that you have applied to a folder, you can change the folder's icon to one that reflects the template type. Follow Steps **1** to **4** to select a template for the main folder, and then click Change Icon. In the Change Icon dialog box, click the icon you want and then click OK.

PUBLISH YOUR IMAGES
to a Web site

You can use the Web Publishing Wizard to publish drawings, photos, and other images to a free Web site.

In the past, if you wanted to show off some photos to family or friends, you had to wait until you got together with them in order to pass around your photo album or prints. Nowadays, it is easy to share a photo immediately with many other people just by attaching the digital version of the image to an e-mail message.

However, what happens if you have many photos that you want to share? Attaching them all to a message or sending multiple messages is impractical, especially if any of your recipients have slower dial-up Internet connections. Placing the digital photos on a Web site and just sending the site address to everyone is a much better solution.

If you do not have a Web site or the know-how to upload images, you can still get your images on the Web. Windows XP's Web Publishing Wizard takes you step-by-step through the process of publishing your images online.

① Connect to the Internet.

② Open the folder that contains the images you want to publish to the Web.

③ Click Publish this folder to the Web.

The Web Publishing Wizard appears.

④ Click Next.

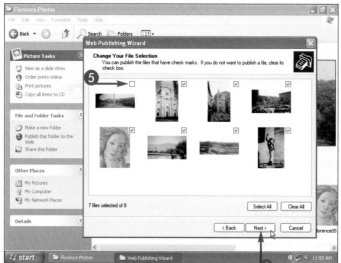

The Change Your File Selection dialog box appears.

⑤ If you do not want to publish a particular image, click its check box (☑ changes to ☐).

⑥ Click Next.

The wizard downloads information about service providers.

52

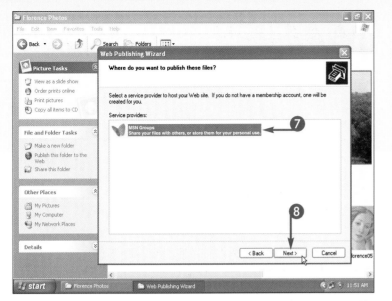

The Where do you want to publish these files dialog box appears.

7 Click MSN Groups.

8 Click Next.

DIFFICULTY LEVEL

Note: If you chose the MSN Groups provider and your Windows XP user account does not have a .NET Passport, a wizard appears so that you can add the Passport to your account.

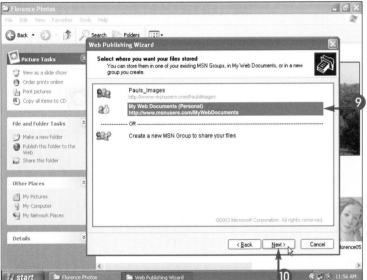

The Select where you want your files stored dialog box appears.

9 Click My Web Documents.

10 Click Next.

Did You Know?

A .NET Passport is really just a Hotmail e-mail account, though more useful because it gives you access to many Microsoft sites, such as the MSN Groups site used in this task. To add a .NET Passport to your user account, click start, Control Panel, and then User Accounts. Click your user name and then click "Set up my account to use a .NET Passport."

Customize It!

Instead of placing all your images in the default My Web Documents folder, you can also create a new folder to hold the images. Follow Steps **1** to **8** to display the "Select where you want your files stored" dialog box. Click the "Create a new MSN Group to share your files" option and then click Next. In the "Create your new group" dialog box, type the group name, click Yes (○ changes to ⊙), click Next, and then follow the rest of the steps in the wizard.

PUBLISH YOUR IMAGES
to a Web site

The Web Publishing Wizard publishes your image to your personal folder on the MSN Groups site. This is a free site for .NET Passport holders that gives you 3MB of space in which to store images or documents. You also have the option of purchasing another 30MB of extra space for a yearly fee.

You can create extra folders in your storage area, add and delete files via the Web, create photo

albums, set up group memberships, send e-mail messages and announcements to the group members, and manage your storage space.

However, if you only want to upload pictures to your MSN group, the Web Publishing Wizard is the only tool you need. It is particularly useful if you are dealing with large images such as photos: The wizard gives you the option of converting the images to the JPEG format, which greatly reduces the file sizes and the upload times.

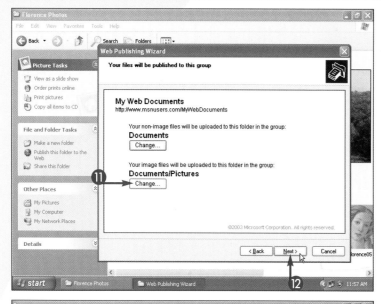

The Your files will be published to this group dialog box appears.

⑪ To change where the wizard stores your images, click Change and use the Change Folders dialog box to select or create another folder.

⑫ Click Next.

The Do you want to adjust picture sizes before publishing dialog box appears.

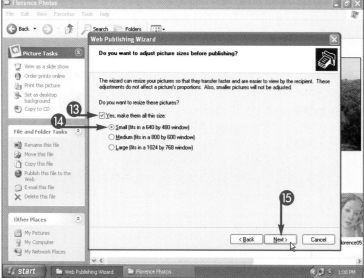

⑬ Click Yes, make them all this size (☐ changes to ☑).

⑭ Click the picture size you prefer (○ changes to ◉).

⑮ Click Next.

The wizard publishes the images to the Web.

Note: You may see a dialog box warning you that image information may be lost. Click Yes to continue.

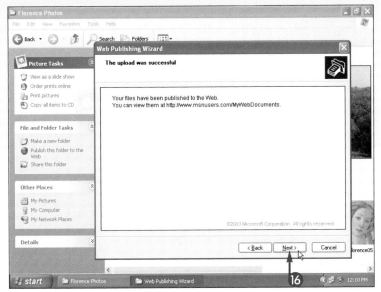

The upload was successful dialog box appears.

⑯ Click Next.

#21 CONTINUED

The Completing the Web Publishing Wizard dialog box appears.

⑰ Click Finish.

The wizard displays the site where you published your images.

⑱ Click the Pictures link to see your pictures.

TIPS

Did You Know?

After you publish images to MSN Groups for the first time, a new My Groups icon is added to your My Network Places folder. My Groups contains subfolders that connect the folders on your MSN Groups site. Instead of using the wizard, you can open these folders and copy images and other files to them directly.

Important!

Although the wizard tells you that your Web site address is www.msnusers.com/ MyWebDocuments, that is not strictly true. On your own computer, Internet Explorer converts this address to www.msnusers.com/ *HotmailAddress*, where *HotmailAddress* is the Hotmail e-mail address associated with your .NET Passport. This is the address to give other people who want to visit your site.

OPEN YOUR IMAGES FOR EDITING
by default

You can force Windows XP to always open an image file in a graphics program for editing when you double-click the file.

For most document types, when you double-click a file, the file opens in an appropriate program for editing. For example, if you double-click a text document, Windows XP opens the file in the Notepad text-editing program; similarly, if you double-click a Rich Text Format document, the file opens in WordPad or Word depending on your computer's settings.

Unfortunately, Windows XP is inconsistent when it comes to graphics files. For example, if you double-click a bitmap image, the file does not open in the

Paint graphics program. Instead, Windows XP loads the file into the Windows Picture and Fax Viewer, which only allows you to view the file; you cannot edit the image. This choice is not only inconsistent, but also frustrating because now you must to close the Windows Picture and Fax Viewer and open the file in Paint.

Fortunately, you can fix the problem by forcing Windows XP to open an image file in Paint or some other graphics program when you double-click the file.

1 Open the folder that contains the images with which you want to work.

2 Click View.

3 Click Details.

4 Click the Type column header to sort the image files by type.

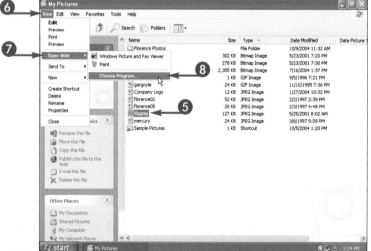

5 Click an image to select it.

6 Click File.

7 Click Open With.

8 Click Choose Program.

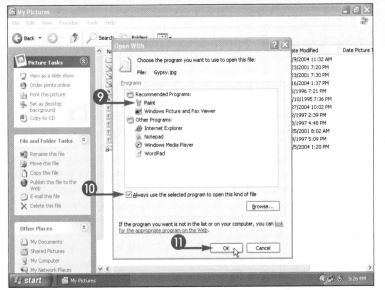

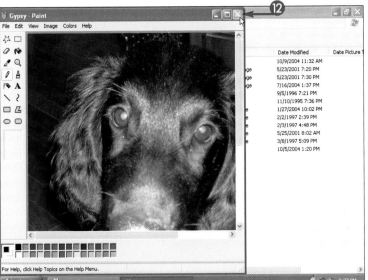

The Open With dialog box appears.

9 Click Paint.

Note: If you have other graphics programs installed on your computer, click the program you prefer to use for editing this file type.

10 Click Always use the selected program to open this kind of file (☐ changes to ☑).

11 Click OK.

Windows XP opens the file in the graphics program.

In this example, Windows will now open all JPEG files in Paint.

12 Click here to close the graphics program.

13 For each of the other graphics file types, repeat Steps **5** to **12** to set the graphics program as the default for that type.

TIPS

Preview It!

If you want to load an image into the Windows Picture and Fax Viewer in the future, you can still do it. Click the image, click File, and then click Preview. To close the Viewer and load the image into Paint, press Ctrl+E.

More Options!

What happens if you have a third-party graphics program that you prefer to use, but the program does not appear in the Programs list of the Open With dialog box? Click Browse and then use the new Open With dialog box to locate the graphics program. Click the program and then click Open.

COMPRESS
your image files

You can compress one or more of your large image files into a smaller format, either to save space or to upload to a Web site.

Image files are often quite large. Complex bitmap images and photo-quality images from a digital camera or scanner run to several megabytes or more. A large collection of such files can easily consume gigabytes of hard drive space. If you are running low on hard drive space, but you do not want to delete any of your image files, compressing those files into smaller versions can help.

Similarly, you may want to upload one or more of your image files to a Web site. You not only have to compress Web images so that users with slow connections can load them in a reasonable time, but you must also convert the images to a format with which all Web browsers can work. The Web Publishing Wizard from Task #21 can compress and convert images before uploading, but the wizard does not work with most Web site providers.

In this task, you learn a trick that enables you to compress images and convert them to the Web-friendly JPEG format.

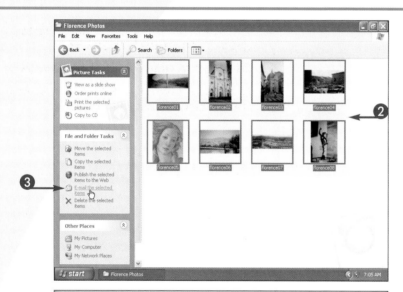

① Open the folder that contains the images you want to compress.

② Select the images.

③ Click E-mail the selected items.

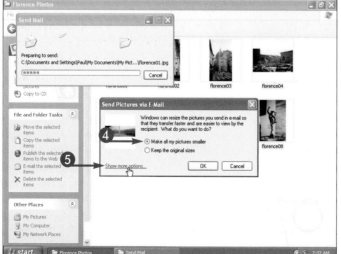

The Send Pictures via E-mail dialog box appears.

④ Click Make all my pictures smaller (○ changes to ⊙).

⑤ Click Show more options.

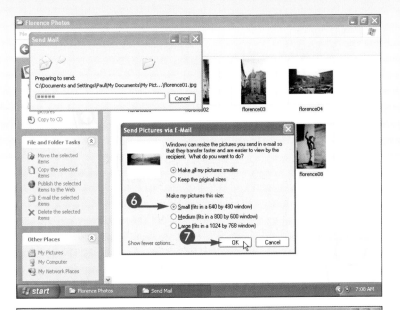

The dialog box expands.

6 Click the picture size you prefer.

7 Click OK.

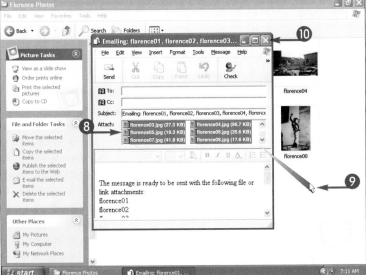

An e-mail message window opens with the compressed and converted images as attachments.

8 Hold down the Ctrl key and click to select each attachment.

9 Click and drag the selected attachments and drop them inside the folder.

10 Click here to close the message window.

The images are now compressed and take up less space on your hard drive.

TIPS

More Options!

If your goal is to save hard drive space, you can place infrequently used images in a compressed folder. This is a special folder that shrinks the images as much as possible. When you want to work with one of the original files, you can extract it from the compressed folder at any time. To create the compressed folder, select the images and then click File, Send To, Compressed (Zipped) Folder. Delete the original images after Windows XP creates the compressed folder.

Check It Out!

For maximum control over compressing image files, you can use a third-party graphics program, such as Paint Shop Pro (available from www.jasc.com) or the free programs IrfanView (www.irfanview.com) or Easy Thumbnails (www.notetab.com).

ADD YOUR OWN NOTES
to an image

You can add text, highlights, and other annotations to certain types of images.

If you collaborate with another person on a text document, you probably communicate with each other by adding notes, suggestions, comments, instructions, and other bits of text in the document. This is better than calling or e-mailing the other person because you can place your text precisely within the document so there is no question about the part of the document to which you are referring.

Windows XP offers a similar capability with images, specifically images saved in the TIFF (or TIF) format. Using the Windows Picture and Fax Viewer program, you can *annotate* a TIFF image, meaning you can add text, highlights, and even notes that look like "sticky notes." So if you are collaborating on an image with another person, or if you simply want to pass along an image with strategically placed comments, you can annotate the image and send it out.

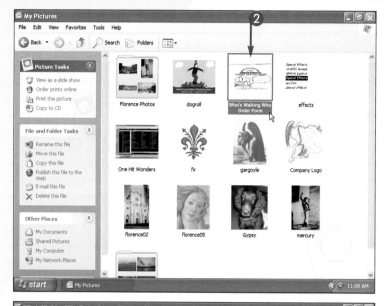

PREVIEW THE IMAGE

1 Open the folder containing the image.

2 Double-click the image.

Note: If you performed Task #22 so that double-clicking opens the image for editing, click File and then Preview instead.

The image appears in the Windows Picture and Fax Viewer.

ADD TEXT TO THE IMAGE

3 Click the New Text Annotation button.

4 Click where you want the text to begin and drag the mouse to create the box.

5 Click inside the box to display the insertion point cursor.

6 Type the text.

7 Click outside the box to set the text.

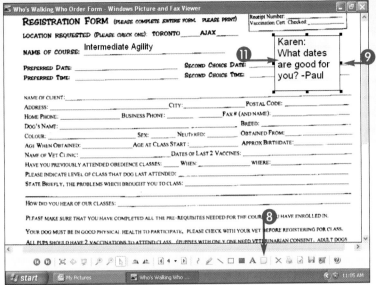

⑧ Click the New Attached
Note Annotation
button.

⑨ Click where you want
the note to begin and
drag the mouse to
create the box.

⑩ Click inside the box to
display the insertion
point cursor.

⑪ Type the text.

⑫ Click outside the box to
set the text.

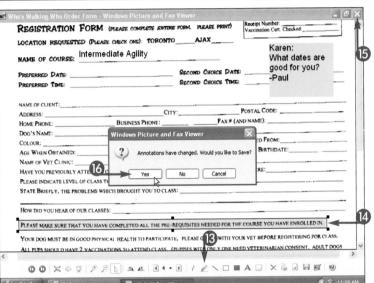

ADD A YELLOW HIGHLIGHT TO THE IMAGE

⑬ Click the New Highlight Annotation
button.

⑭ Click where you want the highlight to
begin and drag the mouse to extend the
highlight.

⑮ Click here to close the image.

⑯ If Windows XP asks if you want to save
your annotations, click Yes.

Windows saves your annotations.

TIPS

More Options!
If you view the image at the default
magnification, your annotations can
be difficult to see. For most images,
you can increase the magnification
to see your work properly. To do this,
click the Zoom In button (🔍) until
the image is the size you want. If you
go too far, click the Zoom Out button
(🔍) to reduce the magnification.

More Options!
Fax images may contain multiple
pages. If so, you can display the page
with which you want to work by
clicking Next Page (▶) and Previous
Page (◀) buttons until the page
appears. You can also click ▾ in the
page list and then click the page you
want.

ADD SOUNDS
to Windows XP events

You can associate sound files with specific Windows XP occurrences, such as minimizing a window or starting a program. This not only adds some aural variety to your system, but it can also help novice users of your computer follow and understand what is happening on the screen.

In Windows XP, a *program event* is an action taken by a program or by Windows XP itself in response to something. For example, if you click a window's Minimize button, the window minimizes to the taskbar. Similarly, if you click an item in a program's menu bar, the menu drops down. Other events, like an error

message, a low notebook battery alarm, or a notification of the arrival of a new e-mail message, are generated internally by a program or by Windows XP.

Windows XP has certain sounds associated with all of these events and many others. Some of these sounds — such as the music you hear when Windows XP starts up — are purely decorative "ear candy." Other sounds — such as the sharp tone that sounds when an error message appears — are more useful. Whether your goal is aural decoration or usefulness, you can augment or change the existing Windows XP sounds.

① Click start.

② Click Control Panel.

The Control Panel window appears.

③ Click Sounds, Speech, and Audio Devices.

The Sounds, Speech, and Audio Devices window appears.

④ Click Change the sound scheme.

62

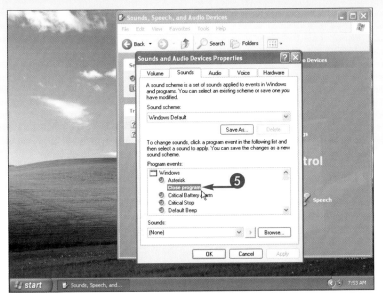

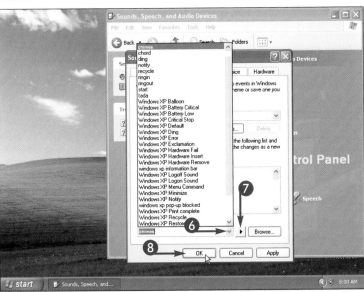

The Sounds and Audio Devices Properties dialog box appears.

⑤ Click the Windows XP event with which you want to work.

⑥ Click here and then click the sound you want to associate with the event.

Note: If the sound you want does not appear in the Sounds list, click Browse and use the Browse For Sound dialog box to choose the sound file you want to use.

⑦ Click here to listen to the sound.

⑧ Click OK.

In this example, the next time you close a program, Windows will play a chimes sound.

TIPS

More Options!
You can save your selected sounds as a *sound scheme*, a collection of sound files associated with Windows XP events. In the Sounds and Audio Devices Properties dialog box, after you have made your sound selections, click Save As, type a name for the sound scheme, and then click OK.

Remove It!
If you tire of your sound scheme and prefer to return Windows XP to its original sound settings, follow Steps **1** to **4** to open the Sounds and Audio Devices Properties dialog box. Click ⌄ in the Sound scheme list and then click Windows Default. If you prefer no sounds at all, click No Sounds and then click OK.

Activate the
MINI PLAYER TOOLBAR

You can control the playback of Windows Media Player, without leaving your current program, by activating and using the Mini Player toolbar.

Many people like to use Windows Media Player as a background program while they do work in another program. For example, they may listen to an audio CD or an Internet radio station while using a word processor or reading and composing e-mail messages.

This works well except when you want to make playback adjustments, such as skipping a track, changing the volume, or pausing the media while you

take a phone call. You must switch from your current program to Windows Media Player, make the adjustments, and then return to your work.

Instead of switching from your current program to Windows Media Player and then back again, you can display the Mini Player toolbar. This toolbar appears on the Windows XP taskbar and enables you to pause playback, skip tracks, mute or change the volume, and even change the playing media. You can also display a small window that shows the current visualization. And if the media you are playing is a video, the same window can also show the video on top of your current window.

1 Right-click an empty section of the taskbar.

2 Click Toolbars.

3 Click Windows Media Player.

Note: The Mini Player toolbar does not appear until you minimize Windows Media Player (see Step 4). You only activate the toolbar once.

4 Click here to minimize the media player.

● The Mini Player Toolbar appears in place of the Windows Media Player taskbar button. You can click these buttons to control the media player:

⏸ Pause/play playing media

⏹ Stop playing media

⏮ Go to previous track

⏭ Go to next track

🔇 Mute the sound

🔊 Display the volume slider

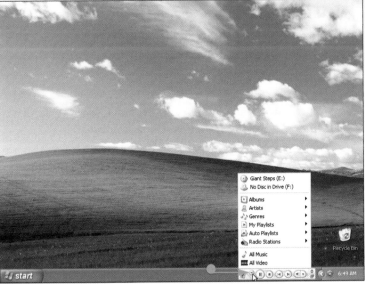

● You can click here to display the Quick Access Panel.

Note: *The Quick Access Panel enables you to change the current media by selecting an audio CD, music album, artist, genre, playlist, or Internet radio station.*

● You can click here to show or hide the Video and Visualization window.

Note: *The Video and Visualization window shows the current visualization (if music is playing) or the current video. The window appears on top of any other window on your screen.*

⑤ Click the Restore button to restore the Windows Media Player window.

The Windows Media Player re-appears.

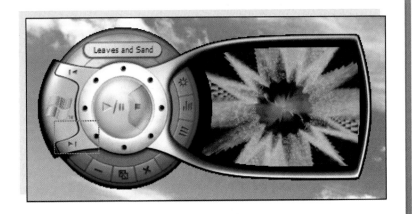

TIPS

More Options!

If you have a large screen, try Windows Media Player's Skin Mode, a smaller version of the player. To activate Skin Mode, press Ctrl+2. To return to Full Mode, press Ctrl+1.

Did You Know?

The Mini Player toolbar's Restore button ( ) is a tiny target that is difficult to click with the mouse. To bypass the mouse and restore Windows Media Player via the keyboard, press Alt+Shift+P.

ADJUST PLAYBACK SETTINGS
for audio and video

You can adjust Windows Media Player's audio and video settings to get the optimal sound and video playback.

For audio playback, Windows Media Player comes with a Graphic Equalizer feature that enables you to adjust the sound quality for the type of media you are playing. Like real-world graphic equalizers, the Windows Media Player version enables you to adjust the gain for different frequencies. If you are not enough of an audiophile to adjust the equalizer appropriately, Windows Media Player also comes with a few dozen default equalizer settings for music genres from Rock and Rap to Country and Classical. You can also adjust the speaker balance.

For video playback, Windows Media Player comes with controls that enable you to adjust the hue, brightness, saturation, and contrast of the video image.

ADJUST AUDIO SETTINGS

① Click the Access Application Menus button.

Note: The Access Application Menus button is new in Windows Media Player 10. You can download the latest version of the program from www.microsoft.com/ windowsmedia.

② Click View.

③ Click Enhancements.

④ Click Graphic Equalizer.

● The Enhancements pane appears and displays the Graphic Equalizer controls.

⑤ Click and drag the sliders to adjust the audio settings.

⑥ To configure the settings for a particular music genre (such as Rock or Jazz), click Default and then click a genre.

⑦ When you have completed your adjustments, click here to close the Enhancements pane.

ADJUST VIDEO SETTINGS

① Click the Access Application Menus button.

② Click View.

③ Click Enhancements.

④ Click Video Settings.

DIFFICULTY LEVEL

● The Enhancements pane appears and displays the Video Settings controls.

⑤ Click and drag the sliders to adjust the video settings.

⑥ When you have completed your adjustments, click here to close the Enhancements pane.

TIPS

More Options!

You can play a video frame-by-frame. Click the Access Application Menus button ([▼]), View, Enhancements, and then Play Speed Settings. In the Enhancements pane, click Next Frame ([●]) and Previous Frame ([●]).

More Options!

You can crossfade one song or audio CD track into another, which gives a smooth audio transition between tunes. Click the Access Application Menus button ([▼]), View, Enhancements, and then Crossfading and Auto Volume Leveling. In the Enhancements pane, click Turn on Crossfading.

DISABLE
CD recording

You can disable Windows Media Player's ability to write audio tracks to a recordable CD, which is useful if you want to prevent others from recording CDs, or if you want to prevent conflicts with other CD recording programs.

Copying files to a recordable CD is called *burning* the CD. This is a useful feature and most people are happy to have it built into Windows XP. However, there are some situations where it pays to disable CD recording, either temporarily or permanently. For example, suppose you have a CD-RW (rewritable) disc in the drive and you are worried that some other user of your computer will accidentally overwrite your

files on the disc. In this case, you could temporarily disable CD recording and then enable it again the next time you use the computer.

As another example, you may be concerned that another user on your computer is burning CDs illegally by, say, copying music files without obtaining a license to do so. Again, you could disable CD recording to thwart this behavior.

Finally, if you have third-party CD-recording software installed on your computer, you may find that Windows XP's recording features interfere with the operation of the program. Disabling XP's CD-recording capability will solve that problem.

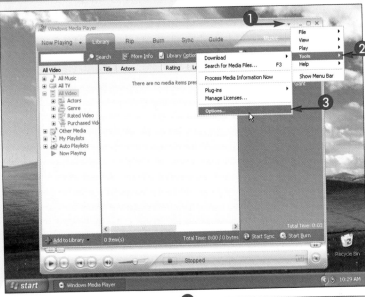

❶ Click the Access Application Menus button.

❷ Click Tools.

❸ Click Options.

The Options dialog box appears.

❹ Click the Devices tab.

❺ Click your recordable CD drive.

❻ Click Properties.

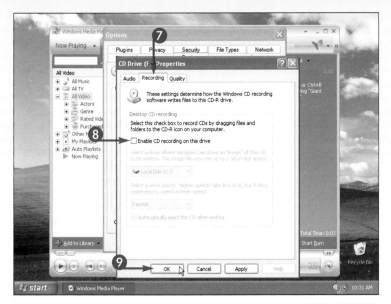

The CD drive's Properties dialog box appears.

⑦ Click the Recording tab.

⑧ Click Enable CD recording on this drive (☑ changes to ☐).

⑨ Click OK to return to the Options dialog box.

 # 28

DIFFICULTY LEVEL

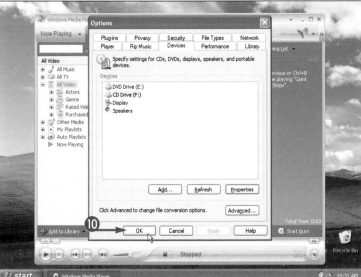

⑩ Click OK.

Windows disables CD recording.

More Options!

If you leave CD recording enabled, you may still not be able to burn a CD if you do not have enough hard drive space. Before copying tracks to the CD, Windows Media Player first creates temporary audio files on your hard drive. These uncompressed files may consume as much as 1GB of hard drive space, so the recording will not work if you do not have enough free space. If you have another drive with enough space, follow Steps **1** to **7** to display the Recording tab. Click ⌄ in the "Select a drive" list and then click the other drive.

More Options!

If you prefer to listen to a music CD you just recorded, tell Windows Media Player not to eject the CD after burning it. Follow Steps **1** to **7** to display the Recording tab, and then click the "Automatically eject CD after recording" option (☑ changes to ☐).

ENABLE PARENTAL CONTROL
for DVDs

You can activate Windows Media Player's Parental Control feature to restrict your children to viewing only DVD movies with a rating at or below a rating that you specify.

If you have DVD decoder software installed on your computer, Windows Media Player can play movies using your DVD drive. This is a great enhancement to Windows XP's multimedia capabilities, but one downside is that not all DVDs are suitable for younger children. If you have kids who use your computer and DVDs that you do not want them to watch, then you can enable Windows Media Player's Parent Control feature. This feature lets you establish a maximum MPAA (Motion Picture Association of

America) rating for children, such as PG or PG-13. Any movie with a higher rating cannot be viewed unless the user knows the correct password.

For Parental Control to work properly, you must use Windows XP's user accounts (see *Teach Yourself VISUALLY Windows XP,* 2nd Edition, to learn how to work with user accounts). First, set up your account with a password. If you have other Administrator accounts on the computer, assign a password to those accounts as well. Next, set up one or more Limited accounts for your children. When they log on using these Limited accounts, Parental Control will not allow them to view DVDs at a rating higher than the one you have specified.

① Click the Access Application Menus button.

② Click Tools.

③ Click Options.

The Options dialog box appears.

④ Click the DVD tab.

Note: If you do not see the DVD tab, then you do not have DVD decoder software installed on your computer. See the tip on the next page to learn how to get a DVD decoder.

⑤ Click Parental control (☐ changes to ☑).

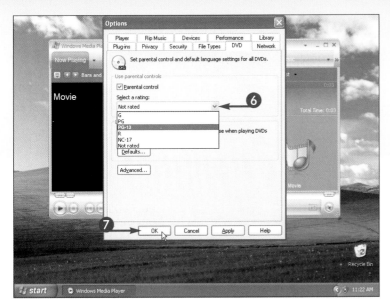

6 Click here and then click the rating you prefer.

Note: The rating you choose is the highest rating that a user can view. For a DVD with a higher rating, only users who log in to Windows XP with an Administrator account can view the movie.

7 Click OK.

Windows Media Player reminds you to set up user accounts.

8 Click OK.

Windows XP activates parental control.

Did You Know?
To find out the rating of a DVD, connect to the Internet and then insert the DVD. In the Now Playing window, click View DVD Info to see data about the disc, including its MPAA rating.

Important!
A number of DVD decoders are available on the market. See the following page for links to some packages that combine DVD and MP3 decoders:
www.microsoft.com/windows/windowsmedia/windowsxp/buypacks.aspx

Get the Most Out of Your Files and Folders

Although you may use Windows XP to achieve certain ends — write memos and letters, create presentations, play games, surf the Internet, and so on — you still have to deal with files and folders as part of your day-to-day work or play. Basic tasks such as copying and moving files, creating and renaming folders, and deleting unneeded files and folders are part of the Windows XP routine.

Your goal should be to make all this file and folder maintenance *less* of a routine so that you have more time during the day to devote to more worthy pursuits. Fortunately, Windows XP offers a number of shortcuts and tweaks that can shorten file and folder tasks and make them more efficient. In this chapter you learn a number of these techniques.

For example, you learn how to open folders and launch files with just a single-click of the mouse instead of the usual double-click. You learn how to open a file in a program other than the one with which it is associated. You learn how to customize the Send To menu to make copying files even faster. You also learn how to make your file searches operate faster; how to move My Documents to another location; how to back up files to a recordable CD; how to work with network files even when you are not logged on to the network; and how to interrupt the printing of a file.

Top 100

Open your files and folders with a
SINGLE CLICK

You can open files and folders more quickly and consistently by customizing Windows XP to open items with a single mouse click instead of a double-click.

Double-clicking is not a difficult skill to learn, but it can be hard to master. Even experienced mouse users — particularly when they are in a hurry — get their timing incorrect or move the mouse slightly so that the double-click does not work. So opening files and folders with a single-click is not only faster but also more efficient. This has the added advantage of making Windows XP more consistent; for example, you already open items on the Start menu with a single-click.

DIFFICULTY LEVEL

More Options!

If you do not like the look of all those underlined files and folders, you can tell Windows XP to turn off the underline except when you point at an icon. Follow Steps **1** to **4** in this task, and then click the "Underline icon titles only when I point at them" option (○ changes to ◉).

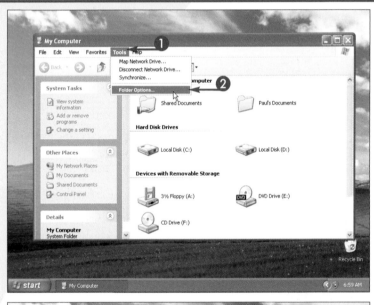

① In any folder window, click Tools.

② Click Folder Options.

The Folder Options dialog box appears.

③ Click the General tab.

④ Click the Single-click to open an item option (○ changes to ◉).

⑤ Click OK.

● Windows XP places an underline under each icon label to remind you to use a single-click.

Open a file with a
DIFFERENT PROGRAM

You can open a file in a different program from the one is normally associated with the file. This enables you to use the other program's features to work on the file.

Every document you create has a particular *file type*. There are Text Documents, Rich Text Documents, Bitmap Images, JPEG Images, and more. All these types have a default program associated with them. For example, Text Documents are associated with Notepad, and Rich Text Documents are associated with WordPad or Word. Double-clicking a file (or single-clicking, if you followed Task #30) opens the file in the associated program. This task shows you how to open the file in another program.

More Options!

Besides opening the file you selected in the new program, you may prefer to open every other file of the same type — such as Text documents or Rich Text Format documents — in the same program. Follow Steps **1** to **6** and then click the "Always use the selected program to open this kind of file" option (☐ changes to ☑).

① Display the folder that contains the file you want to open.

② Click the file.

③ Click File.

④ Click Open With.

● If the program you want to use appears here, click the program and skip the remaining steps.

Note: For some file types, the Open With command may display the Open With dialog box.

⑤ Click Choose Program.

The Open With dialog box appears.

⑥ Click the program you want to use to open the file.

● If the program you want to use does not appear in the list, you can click Browse and use the new Open With dialog box to specify the program.

⑦ Click OK.

Windows XP opens the file in the program you chose.

Add destinations to your
SEND TO MENU

You can enhance the value of the Send To menu, making copying files and folders faster, by customizing the menu with your own destinations.

After you click a file or folder to select it, you can click File and then Send To to reveal Windows XP's Send To menu. This handy menu offers a number of destinations, depending on your computer's configuration: Compressed (Zipped) Folder, Desktop, Mail Recipient, My Documents, and 3½ Floppy (A:). You may also see other removable disk drives, such as a recordable CD drive. When you click one of

these destinations, Windows XP sends a copy of the selected file or folder to that location. This is much faster than copying the item, finding and opening the destination folder, and then pasting the item.

So making a good thing even better by adding your own destinations to the Send To menu is a great idea. You could add a favorite folder, a folder that you use for backup copies, a folder for a current project, a disk drive, the Recycle Bin, or a network folder. You can even add a printer for quick printing to a specific device.

❶ Click start.

❷ Click Run.

The Run dialog box appears.

❸ Type "**C:\Documents and Settings\User\SendTo**", where *User* is your Windows XP user name.

● Your user name appears here.

❹ Click OK.

The SendTo window appears.

● The window shows all the items in the Send To menu, except for your floppy and removable drives.

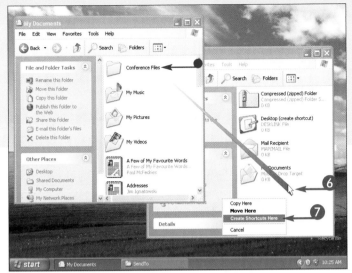

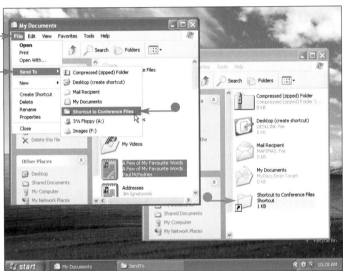

⑤ Open the folder containing the destination you want to add to the Send To menu.

● This example uses Conference Files as the destination folder.

⑥ Right-click and drag the destination item and drop it in the SendTo window.

⑦ Click Create Shortcuts Here from the menu that appears after you drop the item.

● Windows XP adds a shortcut for the destination in the SendTo window.

● The destination now appears in the Send To menu. To view it, you can click any file or folder, File, and then Send To.

TIPS

Customize It!
To add a printer to the Send To menu, click start and then Control Panel. In the Control Panel window, click Printers and Other Hardware, and then click View Installed Printers or Fax Printers. Click and drag the printer to drop it in the SendTo window.

Customize It!
To add a program to the Send To menu, click start, click All Programs, and open the menu that contains an icon for the program. Right-click and drag the program icon to drop it in the SendTo window. Click Copy Here.

Protect a file by making it
READ-ONLY

You can prevent other people from making changes to an important file by designating the file as read-only.

Much day-to-day work in Windows XP is required but not terribly important. Most memos, letters, and notes are run-of-the-mill and do not require extra security. Occasionally, however, you may create or work with a file that *is* important. It could be a carefully crafted letter, a memo detailing important company strategy, or a collection of hard-won brainstorming notes. Whatever the content, such a file requires extra protection to ensure that you do not lose your work.

In Task #82 you learn about setting advanced file permissions that can prevent a document from being changed or even deleted. If your only concern is preventing other people from making changes to a document, a simpler technique you can use is making the document *read-only*. This means that although other people can make changes to a document, they cannot *save* those changes (except to a new file). This task shows you how to make a file read-only.

MAKE A FILE READ-ONLY

1. Open the folder that contains the file with which you want to work.

2. Click the file to select it.

3. Click File.

4. Click Properties.

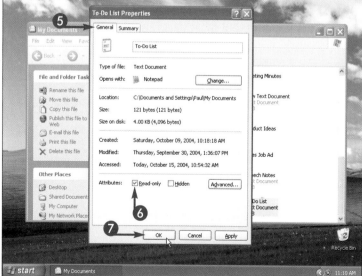

The file's Properties dialog box appears.

5. Click the General tab.

6. Click Read-only (☐ changes to ☑).

7. Click OK.

The file is now read-only.

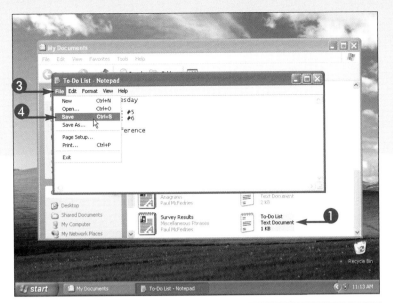

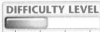

1 Double-click a read-only file to open it.

2 Make changes to the file.

3 Click File.

4 Click Save.

DIFFICULTY LEVEL

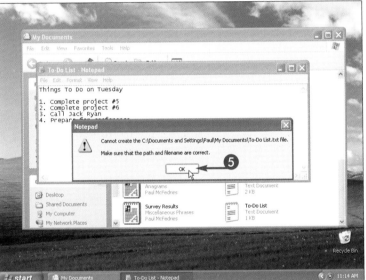

The program tells you it cannot create (save) the file, confirming that the file is read-only.

5 Click OK.

Note: In some programs, the Save As dialog box appears instead. When you click Save, the program displays an "Access Denied" error.

More Options!

Making a file read-only allows other people to view the file, a problem if the file that contains sensitive information such as passwords. To prevent other people from viewing a file, you can hide it. Follow Steps **1** to **5**. Click Hidden (□ changes to ☑), click OK and then press F5. The file icon disappears. To see the file, open the folder containing the file, click Tools and then Folder Options. In the Folder Options dialog box, click the View tab, the "Show hidden files and folders" option (○ changes to ◉), and then OK.

Reverse It!

When you want to make changes to the file yourself, you can remove the read-only attribute. Follow Steps **1** to **5**, click Read-only (☑ changes to □), and then OK.

Make your file searches
RUN FASTER

You can use Windows XP's Indexing Service to create an index of your files, which makes your file searches run noticeably faster.

Having a lot of data is certainly not a bad thing, but *finding* the file you want among all that data can get frustrating. Fortunately, Windows XP's Search feature can help by enabling you to search for files based on name, content, size, and more.

This works well if your computer does not have too many files, but what if your computer has thousands, or even tens of thousands of files (which is not

uncommon these days)? Searching through that many files can take quite a while. To speed things up, you can use Windows XP's Indexing Service to create a *catalog*, or a detailed index of the contents of all your files. Using this catalog, the Search feature can find files up to a hundred times faster than without a catalog. Best of all, the indexing goes on in the background while you are not using your machine, so you can turn on the indexing and then forget about it.

① Click start.

② Click Search.

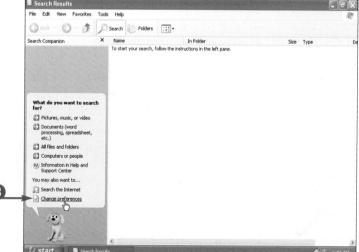

The Search Results window appears.

③ Click Change preferences.

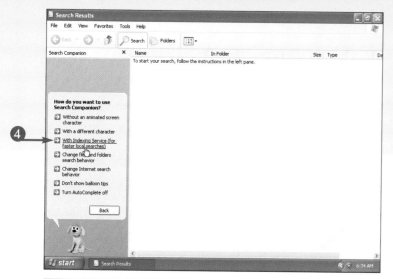

A list of Search Companion preferences appears.

④ Click With Indexing Service.

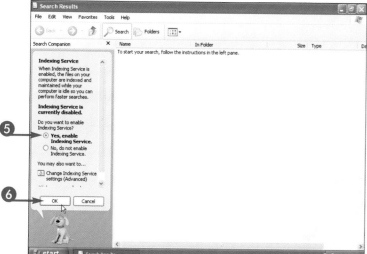

The Indexing Service options appear.

⑤ Click Yes, enable Indexing Service.

⑥ Click OK.

Windows XP begins to index the files on your computer.

Note: Windows XP indexes your files while you are not using your computer. To ensure the indexing completes in a timely manner, activate the service just before your computer will be idle for a while.

Did You Know?

By default, Windows XP includes all of your hard drives in the index catalog. If you do not want a particular hard drive in the catalog, click start, My Computer, click the hard drive, and then click File, Properties. In the General tab of the drive's Properties dialog box, click the "Allow Indexing Service to index this disk for fast file searching" option (☑ changes to ☐).

Caution!

The catalog created by the Indexing Service can use up hundreds of megabytes of disk space. To move the catalog to a hard drive with more space, follow Steps **1** to **4** to display the Indexing Service options. Click the "Change Indexing Service settings" option to display the Indexing Service window. Click the System catalog and then click Action and Properties. Edit the drive letter in the Catalog Location text box, and then click OK.

Move your
MY DOCUMENTS FOLDER

You can move your my Documents folder to another location on your system. This is useful if you want to store your documents on a hard drive with more free space, or if you want to combine My Documents with other data files for easier backups.

By default, your My Documents folder is located in C:\Documents and Settings*User*\My Documents, where *User* is your Windows XP user name (the name that appears at the top of the Start menu). However, when you use My Documents in your everyday work, this location is transparent to you because Windows XP enables you to open the folder

directly, either via the Start menu or via the My Documents link that appears in the task pane of all folder windows.

That feature is convenient, but what if the default location of My Documents becomes a problem? For example, you may find that drive C is running low on hard drive space. Also, many people add to their computer a second hard drive — usually drive D — in which to store their documents. However, having some files in My Documents and others in drive D can be a hassle.

To solve both problems, you can move My Documents to another location.

① Click start.

② Right-click My Documents.

③ Click Properties.

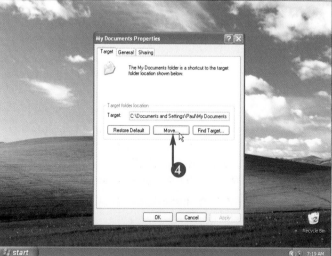

The My Documents Properties dialog box appears.

④ Click Move.

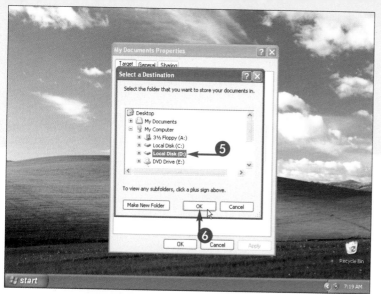

The Select a Destination dialog box appears.

5 Click the hard drive or folder that you want to use as the new location for My Computer.

6 Click OK to return to the My Documents Properties dialog box.

● The new location appears in the Target text box.

7 Click OK to close the My Documents Properties dialog box.

TIPS

Caution!

Do not select a rewritable CD as the location for My Documents because Windows XP does not save files to this location properly. Also, XP does not allow you to copy files directly to My Documents. Instead, you can open the CD in My Computer and copy the files to the CD drive.

Important!

If you have a second hard drive on your computer named, say, drive D, do not make My Documents a subfolder of D. Instead, change the location of My Documents to D:\. This turns the entire hard drive into the My Documents "folder," which gives you easy access to the hard drive and makes backing up all of your data easy (by selecting just My Documents of D in the Backup program).

Back up files to a
RECORDABLE CD

You can use the Backup program to indirectly back up your data to a recordable CD, enabling you to use different CDs for different backup sets, and to store the backups in an offsite location for added safety.

The Backup program that comes with Windows XP (XP Home users must install Backup from the CD) enables you to back up to floppy disks, flash disks, Zip disks, a hard drive location, a network folder, or a tape drive. However, you cannot choose a recordable CD as the backup location.

Fortunately, you can work around this limitation with a simple trick: back up your files to your hard drive and then copy the resulting file to the recordable CD.

This technique makes backups much more useful because CDs are durable and store a relatively large amount of data (about 650MB), and are portable enough to be moved offsite for safekeeping. They are also cheap, so you can use different CDs for different backup sets.

① Start Backup and run through the dialog boxes of the Backup or Restore Wizard until you get to the Backup Type, Destination, and Name dialog box.

② Click here and choose File as the backup type.

③ Type the hard drive location to use as a temporary backup location.

● You can click Browse and navigate to the drive or folder

④ Complete the backup.

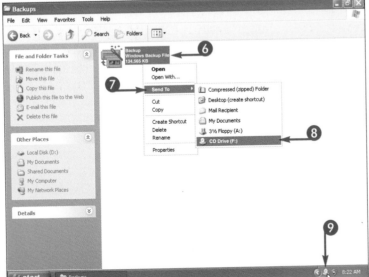

⑤ Open the folder containing the backup file.

⑥ Right-click the backup file.

⑦ Click Send To.

⑧ Click your recordable CD drive.

⑨ Click the icon that appears in the notification area.

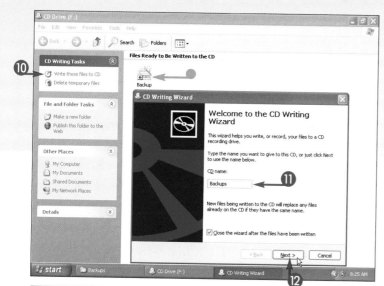

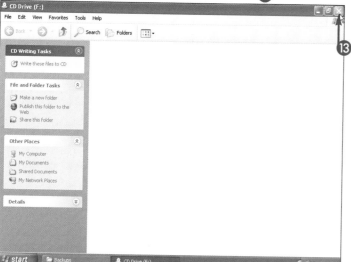

● The backup file appears in the Files Ready to Be Written to the CD area.

⑩ Click Write these files to CD.

The CD Writing Wizard appears.

⑪ Type a name for the CD.

⑫ Click Next.

The Wizard writes the backup files to the CD.

⑬ Click here to close the CD folder.

TIPS

Important!

For this backup trick to work, the backup file you create must be no larger than the 650MB capacity of most recordable CDs. To determine the size of the backup file, run Backup and choose your floppy disk as the location. When the backup begins, the Backup Progress window shows you the Estimated Bytes value. Make a note of this value and then cancel the backup. Adjust your file selections, if necessary, and then run the backup again as described in this task.

Did You Know?

You can restore your backed up files directly from the CD. In the Backup or Restore Wizard, when you get to the What to Restore dialog box, click Browse, open the CD, and then click your backup file.

CHANGE THE DEFAULT ACTION
for a file type

To make your system safer or more efficient, you can change the default action that Windows XP performs when you launch a file.

For each file type (see Task #31), Windows XP defines a *default action*, or what happens to the file when you double-click it. For most file types, the default action is "open," which means the file opens in the program with which the file type is associated.

Changing the default action is useful for some situations. For example, if you often work with video files, you know that playing them in Windows Media

Player is the default action. But you may prefer simply to open the files in Media Player and then start and control the playback from there. Alternatively, certain file types are inherently dangerous. For example, VBScript Script files are small programs that run when you double-click them. A malicious version of such a program can cause damage to your computer, so it is a good idea to change the default action to "edit" (that is, open the file harmlessly in Notepad).

1 Click start.

2 Click My Computer.

The My Computer window appears

3 Click Tools.

4 Click Folder Options.

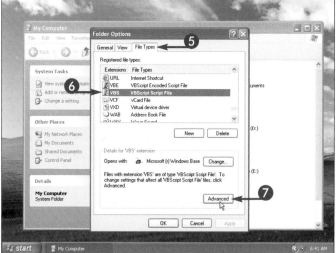

The Folder Options dialog box appears.

5 Click the File Types tab.

6 In the Registered file types list, click the file type with which you want to work.

7 Click Advanced.

Note: If you do not see Advanced, you cannot change the default action for the file type you selected.

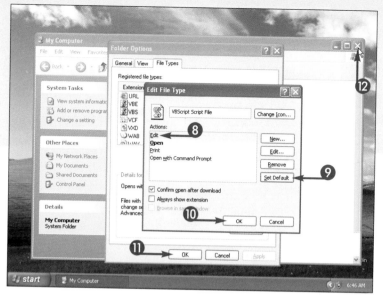

The Edit File Type dialog box appears.

⑧ Click the action that you want to set as the default.

Note: In most cases, the action that is currently the default is shown in bold type.

⑨ Click Set Default.

⑩ Click OK.

⑪ Click OK.

⑫ Click here to close My Computer.

DIFFICULTY LEVEL

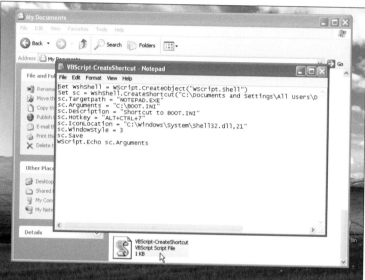

In this example, the default action for VBScript files is changed to Edit. The next time you double-click a VBScript file, it opens in Notepad instead of running.

TIPS

Remove It!

After you change the default type, you can still run the former default action: right-click an example of the file type and then click the action in the shortcut menu. For example, if you know a VBScript file is safe, right-click it and then click Open to run it. To prevent other users from doing this, you can delete the action. Follow Steps **1** to **7**. Click the action and then click Remove. Click Yes to confirm the deletion.

Customize It!

The Edit File Type dialog box also enables you to change the icon associated with a file type. Follow Steps **1** to **7** and then click Change Icon. Use the Change Icon dialog box to select a new icon as described in Task #18.

Work with
NETWORK FILES OFFLINE

You can work with network files and folders even when you are not connected to the network.

One of the main advantages of setting up a small network in your home or office is the ease with which you can share files and folders with other users. You simply share a folder with the network, and other users can use their My Network Places folder to open the shared folder and work with the files.

However, this benefit is lost when you disconnect from the network. For example, suppose you have a notebook computer that you use to connect to the network while you are at the office. When you take

the notebook on the road, you must disconnect from the network. Windows XP enables you to create a dial-up or Internet-based connection to the network, but that is complicated to set up.

Fortunately, you can still get network access of a sort when you are disconnected from the network (or *offline*). Windows XP Professional has an Offline Files feature that enables you to preserve copies of network files on your computer. You can then view and work with these files as though you were connected to the network.

ENABLE OFFLINE FILES

① Turn off Fast User Switching, if it is currently enabled (see the tip on the next page).

② Click start.

③ Click My Computer.

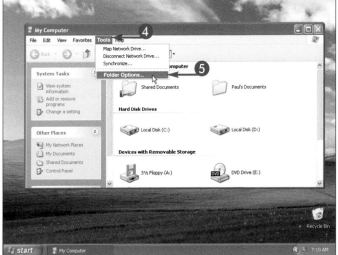

The My Computer window appears.

④ Click Tools.

⑤ Click Folder Options.

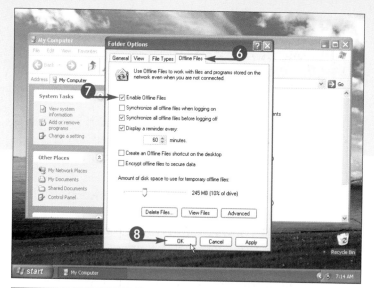

The Folder Options dialog box appears.

6 Click the Offline Files tab.

7 Click Enable Offline Files (□ changes to ☑).

8 Click OK.

You can now make network files available offline.

#38

DIFFICULTY LEVEL

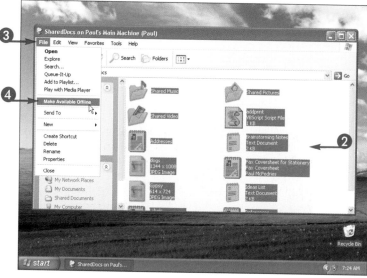

MAKE FILES AVAILABLE OFFLINE

1 Use the My Computer window to open the network folder that contains the files you want to use offline.

2 Select the files you want to use offline.

3 Click File.

4 Click Make Available Offline.

The next time you disconnect from the network, you will still be able to work with the offline files.

Important!

To turn off Fast User Switching, click start, Control Panel, User Accounts, and then the "Change the way users log on or off" option. Click the "Use Fast User Switching" option (☑ changes to □) and then Apply Options.

Did You Know?

The Offline Files feature is not available with Windows XP Home. If you have networked a notebook computer and a desktop computer, consider upgrading the notebook to Windows XP Professional. This enables you to use the desktop computer's shared files offline. Note that you do not need to upgrade the desktop computer to Windows XP Professional for this to work.

Work with
NETWORK FILES OFFLINE

With the Offline Files feature enabled, you can choose which shared files and folders you want to work with offline.

Windows XP creates a special Offline Files Folder that contains all the shared network files that you choose to work with offline. Although you cannot delete and rename the offline files, you can open and edit the files just as though you were connected to the network. When you reconnect to the network,

Windows XP automatically *synchronizes* the files. This means that Windows XP does two things: First, it updates your Offline Files Folder by creating copies of any new or changed files in the shared network folder. Second, it updates the shared network folder with the files you changed while you were offline. This synchronization occurs automatically when you log on to the network and when you log off the network.

The Offline Files Wizard appears.

Note: *The Offline Files Wizard only appears the first time you make a file or folder available offline. In the future, you need only perform Steps 1 to 4 of Make Files Available Offline in the previous task.*

5 Click Next.

6 Click Automatically synchronize the Offline Files when I log on and log off my computer.

7 Click Next.

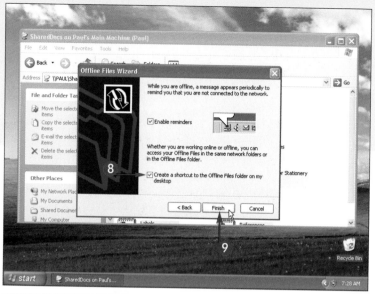

8 Click Create a shortcut to the Offline Files folder on my desktop (□ changes to ☑).

9 Click Finish.

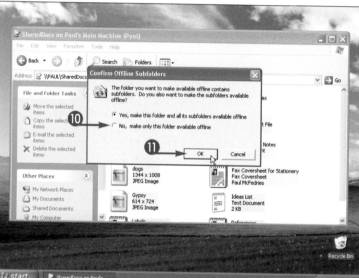

If the offline folder contains subfolders, the Confirm Offline Subfolders dialog box appears.

10 If you do not want to use the subfolder offline, click No, make only this folder available offline.

11 Click OK.

Windows XP synchronizes the offline files.

You can now disconnect from the network and work with the files offline.

Important!

When Windows XP synchronizes your offline files, it may find that a file has been changed both on the network share and on your offline computer. In that case, you see the Resolve File Conflicts dialog box, which gives you three options: keep the network version of the file (you lose your offline changes); keep the offline version of the file (you lose the network changes); or keep both versions (the offline version is saved under a modified filename).

Did You Know?

You can also synchronize the offline files yourself. In any folder window, click Tools and then click Synchronize to display the Items to Synchronize dialog box. If you do not want a particular network folder synchronized, click its check box (☑ changes to □). Click Synchronize.

Chapter 4: Get the Most Out of Your Files and Folders 91

INTERRUPT PRINTING
a file

You can send a command to Windows XP to pause printing a particular file or all the pending print jobs. This is useful if you want to change printer properties, load different paper in the printer, or cancel one or more print jobs.

When you print a document, the program sends the document to Windows XP's printing system, which then configures the file for printing and coordinates the print job with the printer. This normally happens behind the scenes, and you rarely have to participate until you remove the printout from the printer. However, there may be times when you intervene in

a pending print job. For example, you may realize that you need to load different paper into the printer. Similarly, you may want to adjust some printer properties, such as changing the page layout or the printer's paper source. Also, you may have sent a file to the printer and then realize that you do not want it printed after all.

For these and similar situations, you can interrupt the printing process, which means pausing or canceling the printing of a particular file, or pausing or canceling all pending print jobs.

VIEW PENDING PRINT JOBS

1 Print the file.

● The printer icon appears in the taskbar's notification area.

2 Double-click the printer icon.

A window for the printer appears.

● This list shows the pending print jobs (the *print queue*).

Note: *Windows XP can send documents to the printer very quickly. Unless the file is quite large, you may see your document in the print queue for only a short time.*

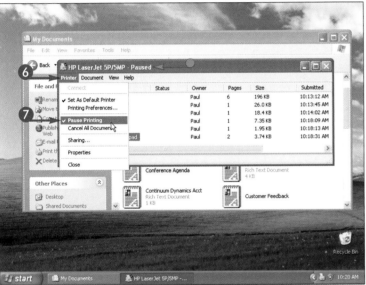

PAUSE A DOCUMENT

③ Click the document you want to pause.

④ Click Document.

⑤ Click Pause.

● Windows XP adds the word *Paused* to the document's Status column.

Note: *To continue printing, click the file, Document, and then Resume.*

39

DIFFICULTY LEVEL

PAUSE THE PRINTER

⑥ Click Printer.

⑦ Click Pause Printing.

● Windows XP adds the word *Paused* to the window title bar.

Note: *To continue printing, click Printer and then Pause Printing.*

More Options!

If you do not want a file printed after all, click the file in the print queue, Document, and then Cancel. Click Yes when Windows XP asks you to confirm the cancellation. To remove all the files from the print queue, click Printer and then Cancel All Documents. Click Yes to confirm.

Did You Know?

You can buy yourself a bit more time to work with print jobs by slowing down the way Windows XP *spools* files (sends the pages to the printer). Click Printer and then click Properties. In the printer's Properties dialog box, click the Advanced tab and then click the "Start printing after last page is spooled" option (○ changes to ⊙). Click OK.

5

Maximize Your Internet Connections

It has been over a decade since the Internet began its move into the mainstream, and it is now firmly entrenched there. In fact, most households in the developed world have Internet access, and rarely does a business not offer its employees the benefits of e-mail, the World Wide Web, and other Net services.

Having Internet access is one thing, but using the Internet efficiently is quite another. If you use any part of the Internet regularly, there are many tips and techniques you can learn to make your online work or play faster, safer, or more useful. This chapter is the first of four in this book that cover Internet-related topics. Your focus in this chapter is on the most basic aspect of the Internet experience: the connection. Whether you use a dial-up or a

broadband Internet Service Provider (ISP), you will find lots of tasks geared toward improving your Internet connections.

If you are a dial-up user, you learn how to specify an alternate phone number (just in case the main number is unavailable); how to use area code rules; and how to turn off those annoying sounds your modem makes while connecting.

For both dial-up and broadband use, you also learn the fastest way to connect to your ISP; how to share your connection on your network; and how to disconnect automatically after your connection has been idle for a while. For broadband connections only, you learn how to display an alert whenever your connection is not performing up to speed.

Top 100

Connect to the Internet
AUTOMATICALLY

You can set up your dial-up or broadband Internet connection to connect automatically when you launch an Internet program or double-click the connection icon.

Whether you use dial-up or broadband, when you launch an Internet program or double-click the connection icon, Windows XP displays the Connect dialog box. This dialog box gives you the opportunity to adjust the connection specifics in some way, such as changing the user name or password, typing a

new dial-up phone number, and so on. In reality, however, most people never change anything in this dialog box. They simply click Dial and proceed with the connection.

If that is the case with your own connection, you can avoid the unnecessary step of opening the Connect dialog box. In this task, you learn how to do that by telling Windows XP that you do not want to be prompted for a name, password, and phone number.

① Double-click the Internet connection shortcut on the desktop.

Note: If you do not have a connection icon on your desktop, click start, All Programs, Accessories, Communications, Network Connections, and then double click the Internet connection icon.

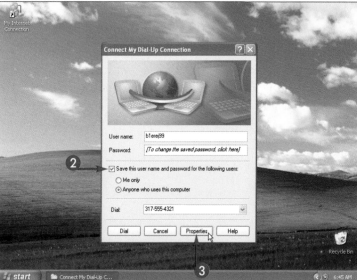

The Internet connection's Connect dialog box appears.

② Click Save this user name and password for the following users (☐ changes to ☑).

③ Click Properties.

The connection's Properties dialog box appears.

④ Click Prompt for name and password, certificate, etc. (☑ changes to ☐).

⑤ Click Prompt for phone number (☑ changes to ☐).

⑥ Click OK.

DIFFICULTY LEVEL

● Windows XP connects automatically to the Internet.

TIPS

Desktop Trick!

You can make connecting to the Internet even easier by placing your dial-up connection in a more convenient spot. To put a shortcut for the connection on your desktop, click start, All Programs, Accessories, Communications, and Network Connections. Right-click the dial-up connection, click Create Shortcut, and then click Yes when Windows XP asks if you want the shortcut on your desktop. Alternatively, see Task #14 to learn how to add the Connect To menu to your Start menu.

Reverse It!

If your connection properties change and you need to display the Connect dialog box again, click start, All Programs, Accessories, Communications, and Network Connections. Right-click the connection icon and then click Properties. Follow Steps **4** to **6** in this task.

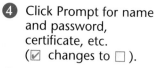

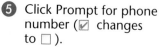

Add an
ALTERNATE ISP PHONE NUMBER

You can set up your dial-up connection with one or more alternate phone numbers to use if the main dial-up number does not work.

Connecting to your ISP is usually smooth and trouble-free, but not always. If all the ISP's modems are tied up, you will receive a busy signal. If there is some technical problem on the ISP's end, your call will not go through. There are, in fact, a number of ways that the connection process can go awry.

One way to fix such a problem is to dial a different phone number. Most major ISPs offer alternate

numbers, and trying one of these other numbers is often enough to make the connection. However, having to look up the alternate number and then enter it in the Connect dialog box is a pain, particularly if you followed Task #40 and now bypass that dialog box. However, Windows XP enables you to store one or more alternate numbers with the connection, and Windows XP will tries those numbers automatically if a problem occurs with the main number.

① Double-click the Internet connection shortcut on the desktop to display the Connect dialog box.

② Click Properties.

Note: If you followed Task #40 to bypass the Connect dialog box, click start, All Programs, Accessories, Communications, and Network Connections. Right-click the connection icon and then click Properties.

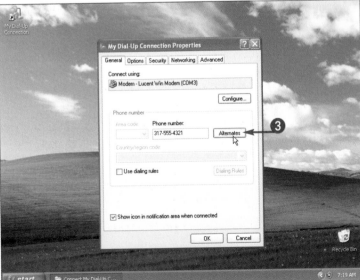

The connection's Properties dialog box appears.

③ Click Alternates.

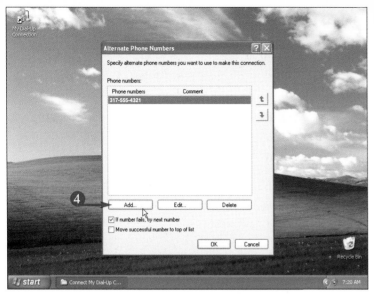

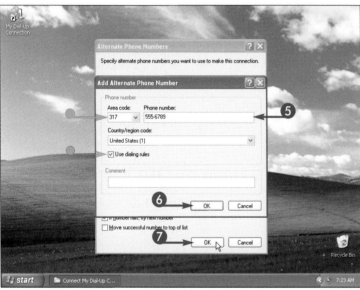

The Alternate Phone Numbers dialog box appears.

④ Click Add.

The Add Alternate Phone Number dialog box appears.

⑤ Type the phone number.

● You can click Use dialing rules (☐ changes to ☑) to include the area code.

● You can type the area code here.

⑥ Click OK.

⑦ Click OK.

Windows saves the alternate phone number.

TIPS

More Options!

If you find that one of the alternate phone numbers is more reliable, you can move it to the top of the phone number list. In the Alternate Phone Numbers dialog box, click the number and then click ⬆ until the number is at the top. You can also click ⬆ to set up the list the way you want. Alternatively, have Windows XP manage this for you automatically by clicking Move successful number to top of list (☐ changes to ☑).

More Options!

If you need to change a phone number, follow Steps 1 to 3 to display the Alternate Phone Numbers dialog box. Click the number, click Edit, and then use the Edit Alternate Phone Number dialog box to change the number. If you no longer need a number, click it and then click Delete.

Dial using
AREA CODE RULES

You can configure your dial-up connection to use the appropriate area code rules that apply to your phone system.

Many phone systems — particularly those in major metropolitan areas — are implementing increasingly confusing area code rules. For example, when you phone a number in the same area code, some phone systems insist that you include the area code. In some cases, these are long-distance calls, so you even have to dial a 1 (or some other country or region code) to start the call.

Similarly, in some larger cities, the phone company has actually run out of numbers in the main area code, so they have created a whole new area code for the city. These are not usually long-distance calls, however, so even though you have to include the area code, you do not usually have to dial a 1 to get started.

To make things worse, in both cases the area code may apply only to certain phone number prefixes. (The prefix is the first three digits of the seven-digit number.) If your ISP's number falls into any of these categories, you can define a new area code rule to handle it.

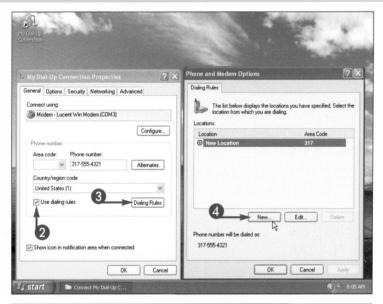

① Follow Steps **1** to **2** in Task #41 to display your Internet connection's Properties dialog box.

② Click Use dialing rules (☐ changes to ☑).

③ Click Dialing Rules.

The Phone and Modem Options dialog box appears.

④ Click New.

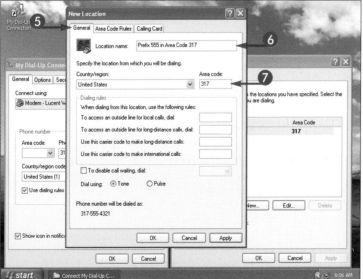

The New Location dialog box appears.

⑤ Click the General tab.

⑥ Type a name for the new location.

⑦ Type the area code from which you will be dialing.

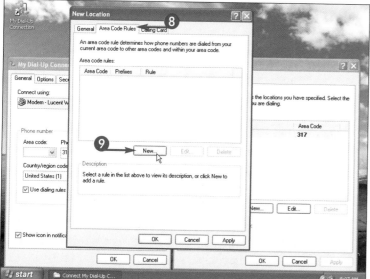

8 Click the Area Code Rules tab.

9 Click New.

The New Area Code Rule dialog box appears.

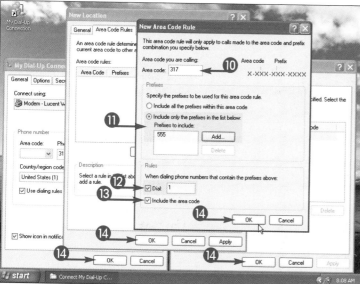

10 Type your area code.

11 If the rule applies only to specific prefixes, click here (○ changes to ◉), click Add, and type the prefix.

12 To dial a country code, click Dial (□ changes to ☑) and type the code.

13 To dial the area code, click here (□ changes to ☑).

14 Click OK in each dialog box.

Windows saves the new area code rules.

TIPS

Did You Know?
If all you need is 10-digit dialing — that is, the area code and phone number — you do not need to set up a special area code rule. Instead, just type the 10-digit phone number in the Dial text box of the Connect dialog box.

Check It Out!
To use your new area code rule, display your Internet connection's Connect dialog box. You will see a new Dialing from list. Click ▾ in that list and then click the name of the new location you created in this task.

ACCESS AN OUTSIDE LINE

You can set up your modem to dial a number — such as 9 — to access an outside line. This is useful if you are connecting to the Internet from an office or hotel.

Large organizations, such as a corporation or hotel, may contain hundreds or even thousands of offices or rooms, all with telephones. It would cost a small fortune to give each phone its own line. In most cases, these organizations set up a *private branch exchange* (or PBX), which enables users to make internal calls to each other, usually by dialing a 3- or

4-digit number. The PBX is typically wired up to just a few outside lines that all users must share. To access one of these outside lines, you must dial a number, usually 9 for local calls and 8 for long-distance calls.

If you find yourself visiting an organization that uses a PBX, you may need to access the Internet through your notebook computer. If so, then you can configure your modem to dial the appropriate number to access an outside line.

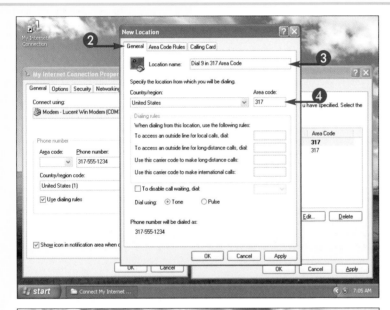

① Follow Steps **1** to **4** in Task #42 to display the New Location dialog box.

② Click the General tab.

③ Type a name for the new location.

④ Type the area code from which you will be dialing.

⑤ Type the number you need to dial for an outside line on a local call.

⑥ Type the number you need to dial for an outside line on a long-distance call.

⑦ Click OK.

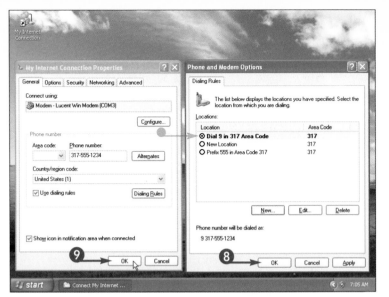

- The new location appears in the Locations list.

⑧ Click OK.

⑨ Click OK.

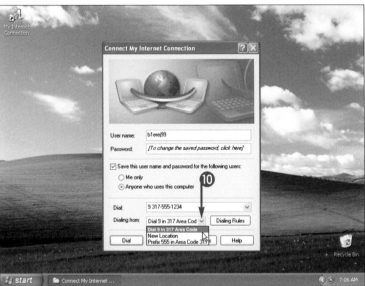

⑩ To use the new location, click here and then click the location.

Windows dials using the access number.

TIPS

More Options!

The tones that call waiting uses to announce an incoming call can disrupt a modem that is connected to the Internet. Therefore, you should disable call waiting prior to connecting. In the Phone and Modem Options dialog box, click the location you want to use and then click Edit. Click the "To disable call waiting, dial" option (☐ changes to ☑), click ☑, and then click the appropriate code for disabling call waiting (such as *70).

More Options!

If you use a carrier to make long-distance calls, you must dial the company's carrier code before connecting. Display the New Location dialog box (or edit an existing location) and type the code in the "Use this carrier code to make long-distance calls" box. If you have a separate carrier code for international calls, you can type that in as well.

Turn off your
MODEM'S SOUNDS

To avoid disrupting or annoying those nearby, you can turn off the noises that your modem makes while it connects to the Internet.

When you launch your dial-up connection, your modem first dials your ISP's number. On the ISP's side, the incoming call is routed to a bank of modems and the first available modem takes the call. That modem then routes your call to the ISP's main Internet connection, and you see the "now connected" message and the connection icon in your taskbar.

Between the dialing portion and the connection, you hear some loud and not particularly pleasant noises coming from your modem. Modems use tones to send information, so that racket you hear is the result of the tones being sent back and forth when your modem arranges for an Internet connection with your ISP's modem. This can occasionally be useful; for example, not hearing the tones tells you that something is wrong with the connection process. However, most of the time you probably do not need to hear the tones. As you see in this task, Windows XP enables you to turn off your modem's sounds.

① Click start.

② Click Control Panel.

The Control Panel window appears.

③ Click Printers and Other Hardware.

The Printers and Other Hardware dialog box appears.

④ Click Phone and Modem Options.

Note: You can also follow Steps 1 to 3 in Task #42 to display the Phone and Modem Options dialog box.

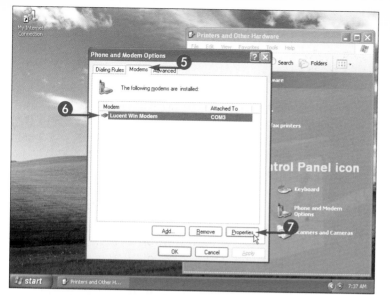

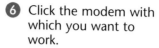

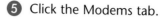

The Phone and Modem Options dialog box appears.

5 Click the Modems tab.

6 Click the modem with which you want to work.

7 Click Properties.

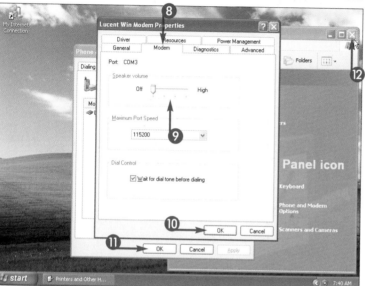

The modem's Properties dialog box appears.

8 Click the Modem tab.

9 Click and drag the slider all the way to the left (Off).

10 Click OK to return to the Phone and Modem Options dialog box.

11 Click OK.

12 Click here to close the Control Panel.

The next time you connect to the Internet, you will not hear your modem's sounds.

TIPS

More Options!

If you are having trouble connecting to the Internet, there may be a problem with your modem. To check this, follow Steps **1** to **7** to display the modem's Properties dialog box. Click the Diagnostics tab and then click Query Modem. If Windows XP cannot communicate with the modem, then you have a problem. If the modem is external, make sure it is turned on and connected correctly. If the modem is internal, you can take it to a computer shop for repair or replacement.

More Options!

For quicker connections, you can make your modem dial faster. Follow Steps **1** to **7** to display the modem's Properties dialog box. Click the Advanced tab and type **ATS11=40** in the Extra Initialization Commands text box. For even faster dialing, you can try numbers less than 40, but dialing too fast may cause connection problems.

SHARE YOUR CONNECTION
on the network

You can set up your Internet connection so that other people on your network can use it. This saves money because multiple users can share a single Internet connection, and it saves time because you have to configure just one connection.

If you have multiple computers at home or in a small office, one conundrum you may be facing is how to give each user Internet access. For dial-up, the most obvious way to do this is to configure each computer to use the same connection, but split the phone line among all the modems. That works, but splitting the

phone line means that only one person can use it at a time, which just leads to problems. For broadband, some ISPs do not allow multiple users to connect at the same time, and for those that do, you still must supply each user with a proper modem, which is an expensive proposition.

To solve all these problems, Windows XP's Internet Connection Sharing (ICS) feature enables you to share a single Internet connection with multiple users over a network.

1. Click start.
2. Click All Programs.
3. Click Accessories.
4. Click Communications.
5. Click Network Connections.

The Network Connections window appears.

6. Click your Internet connection.
7. Click File.
8. Click Properties.

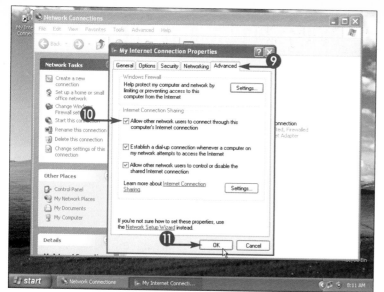

The Internet connection's Properties dialog box appears.

Note: You can also display the Internet connection's Properties dialog box by following Steps 1 to 2 in Task #41.

45

DIFFICULTY LEVEL

⑨ Click the Advanced tab.

⑩ Click Allow other network users to connect through this computer's Internet connection (☐ changes to ☑).

⑪ Click OK to return to the Network Connections window.

● Your Internet connection icon now displays "Shared" in the description, indicating that multiple users can share the same connection.

⑫ Click here to close the Network Connections window.

TIPS

More Options!
To prevent users from modifying and even disabling ICS on your computer, follow Steps **1** to **9** to display the Advanced tab of the Internet connection's Properties dialog box, click the "Allow other network users to control or disable the shared Internet connection" option (☑ changes to ☐), and then click OK.

More Options!
If you prefer to control when you establish the dial-up connection, follow Steps **1** to **9** to display the Advanced tab of the Internet connection's Properties dialog box, click the "Establish a dial-up connection whenever a computer on my network attempts to access the Internet" option (☑ changes to ☐), and then click OK.

Important!
To prevent Internet-based intruders from accessing your network when ICS is enabled, be sure to turn on the Windows Firewall. See Task #48 for details.

DISCONNECT AUTOMATICALLY
after your computer has been idle

If your dial-up connection charges by the hour, or ties up your phone line, you can force Windows XP to disconnect automatically whenever the connection has been idle for a certain time.

Many ISPs have dial-up accounts that offer a certain number of hours of connection time per month. After you have exceeded those hours, however, the company charges your account at an hourly rate. This is a reasonable trade-off if you happen to have a great deal of work (or play) to do on the Internet in a particular month. It is not so great if you run up

connection time by forgetting to disconnect at the end of the day and the connection remains active overnight.

Forgetting to disconnect is also a problem if your dial-up connection goes through the same phone line that you use for voice calls. You could miss one or more important calls because the line remains busy while your Internet connection is active.

To avoid unnecessary connection charges and missed phone calls, you can tell Windows XP to disconnect automatically when your connection has been idle for a specified amount of time.

❶ Click start.

❷ Click All Programs.

❸ Click Accessories.

❹ Click Communications.

❺ Click Network Connections.

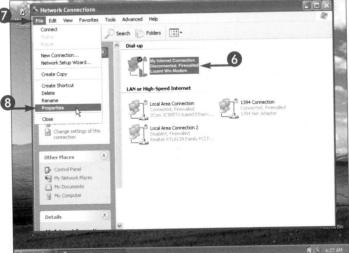

The Network Connections window appears.

❻ Click your Internet connection.

❼ Click File.

❽ Click Properties.

The Internet connection's Properties dialog box appears.

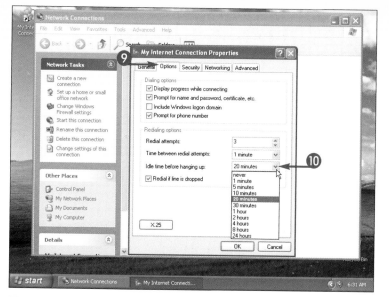

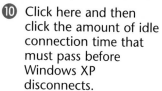

Note: You can also display the Internet connection's Properties dialog box by following Steps 1 to 2 in Task #41.

⑨ Click the Options tab.

⑩ Click here and then click the amount of idle connection time that must pass before Windows XP disconnects.

Note: If you prefer to keep your connection active all the time, click "never" in the list.

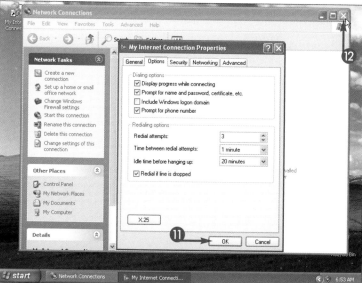

⑪ Click OK.

⑫ Click here to close the Network Connections window.

Windows will now disconnect your connection after the amount of time you specified.

TIPS

More Options!

The opposite problem occurs when you inadvertently lose your Internet connection. This can happen due to noise on the phone line, call waiting beeps, or a glitch on the ISP's end. To ensure that Windows XP reconnects when the connection goes down in this way, follow Steps 1 to 9 and click the "Redial if line is dropped" option (☐ changes to ☑).

More Options!

If you have trouble connecting to your ISP, Windows XP redials up to three times, with one minute between each redial. To change these options, follow Steps 1 to 9. Click the "Redial attempts" spin box to change the number of times Windows XP redials. Also, consider increasing the time between redials by clicking ☑ in the "Time between redial attempts" list and then clicking a time interval.

SEE AN ALERT
when your broadband connection has a problem

You can have Windows XP display an alert if your broadband connection goes down or becomes slow.

Broadband Internet connections tend to be of the set-it-and-forget-it type. That is, you connect when you turn your computer on, and then you leave the connection active until you turn your computer off. (If you are curious about how long your connection has been active, click the connection icon in the taskbar's notification area. This displays the connection's Status dialog box, which, among other things, tells you the duration that the connection has

been active.) This "always on" aspect of broadband means that it is often taken for granted, but broadband connections can have problems. Trouble at the ISP's end, noise on the line, a modem malfunction, or even an accidentally unplugged cable can all slow down or even shut down your broadband link. When this happens, it helps to find out as soon as possible so that you can take some action, such as shutting down and restarting the modem or checking the cable. Windows XP can display an alert upon detecting that the connection has a problem.

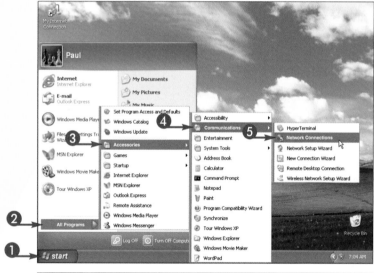

① Click start.

② Click All Programs.

③ Click Accessories.

④ Click Communications.

⑤ Click Network Connections.

The Network Connections window appears.

⑥ Click the network connection that leads to your broadband modem.

⑦ Click Change settings of this connection.

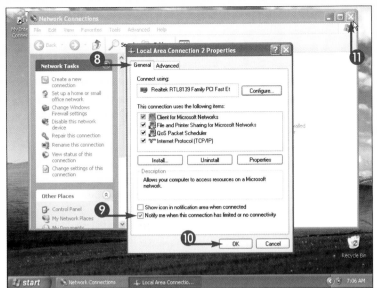

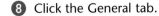
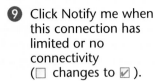

The connection's Properties dialog box appears.

8 Click the General tab.

9 Click Notify me when this connection has limited or no connectivity (☐ changes to ☑).

10 Click OK.

11 Click here to close the Network Connections window.

 # 47

DIFFICULTY LEVEL

● If a problem occurs with your broadband connection, this icon and a message appear in the taskbar's notification area.

TIPS

Did You Know?

If you have a problem with your broadband connection, turn off the modem for a minute or so, and then turn it back on. If this does not solve the problem, follow Steps **1** to **6** and then click the "Repair this connection" option. Windows XP runs through a series of steps in an attempt to fix the problem. Note that this repair feature is available for any network connection.

Customize It!

When it sets up the connections for your computer's network cards, Windows XP provides uninformative and therefore easily confusing names such as Local Area Connection and Local Area Connection 2. To avoid confusion, you can rename the broadband connection (to, say, Broadband Connection). Follow Steps **1** to **6**, click the "Rename this connection" option, type the new name, and press Enter.

Chapter 6

Enhance Internet Security and Privacy

The Internet is now the online home away from home for hundreds of millions of people around the world. The lure of all that information, entertainment, and camaraderie has proven to be simply impossible to resist.

But the Internet has also lured more than its fair share of another class of people: malicious hackers, system intruders, and con artists of every stripe. These miscreants seem to spend most of their waking hours thinking up new ways to disrupt the Internet, break into your online computer, and steal everything from your credit card number to your full identity. Thankfully, like crime in the real world, online crime is still relatively rare. However, as the

newspaper headlines attest almost daily, cybercrime is a big business, and so it pays to play safe.

This chapter helps by offering you a full suite of tasks and techniques designed to make your Internet sessions as safe as possible. You learn how to keep intruders out of your system; how to guard your Internet passwords; how to restrict Internet content; how to reduce spam; and how to use e-mail and Web media safely and securely. Maintaining your privacy while online is an important issue as well, so you also learn in this chapter how to keep your e-mail activities private and how to erase your tracks when you play Internet media.

Top 100

Protect your computer from
INTERNET INTRUDERS

You can ensure that another person cannot infiltrate your system while you are connected to the Internet by turning on the Windows Firewall.

Computers "talk" to the outside world through the use of *ports*, which are usually physical attachment points. For example, the places on the back of your computer where you plug in your mouse, keyboard, and printer are all ports. But computers also have nonphysical ports that are maintained by Windows XP. These ports enable information to be exchanged over the Internet. For example, World Wide Web data uses one port, the File Transfer Protocol (FTP) uses another, and e-mail uses two different ports, one each for incoming and outgoing messages.

Unfortunately, the world's hackers have figured out a way to use these ports for their own nefarious purposes. If malicious users detect an undefended port on your computer while you are online, they can use that port to break into your system. This happens all the time, particularly for always-on broadband connections. To protect your system from these intrusions, you can block your ports by activating the Windows Firewall.

1 Click the Windows Security Alerts icon in the taskbar's notification area.

Note: *If you do not see the Windows Security Alerts icon, click start, All Programs, Accessories, System Tools, and then Security Center.*

The Security Center window appears.

2 Click Windows Firewall.

Note: *If the Firewall setting is "On" in the Security Center window, you do not need to complete the rest of these steps.*

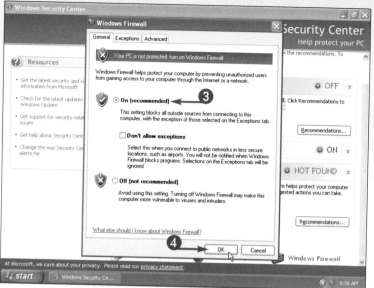

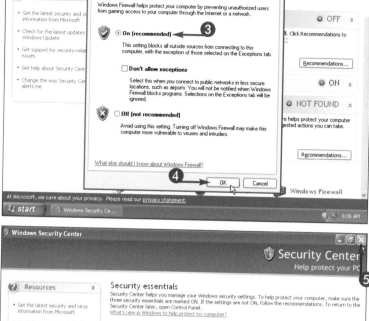

The Windows Firewall dialog box appears.

③ Click On (○ changes to ⊙).

④ Click OK.

DIFFICULTY LEVEL

● In the Security Center window, the Firewall setting changes to On.

⑤ Click here to close the Security Center window.

TIPS

Check It Out!

The Windows Firewall provides adequate protection from online intrusions. However, much better third-party firewall products are available. One of the best and most popular is ZoneAlarm, which is available from www.zonelabs.com.

Did You Know?

The Windows Security Alerts icon (⬚) only appears if you have Windows XP Service Pack 2 installed. For other XP versions, click start, Control Panel, Network and Internet Connections, and then Network Connections. Right-click your Internet connection and then click Properties. Click Advanced and then click "Protect my computer and network by limiting or preventing access to this computer from the Internet" (☐ changes to ☑). Click OK.

PREVENT ADS
from appearing on your computer

You can prevent online users from sending one type of unsolicited advertising message that goes directly to your computer by shutting down a little-used Windows XP service.

On large networks, administrators sometimes send a message to some or all of the users. For example, if the network must be shut down for an upgrade, the administrator would send a message in advance so that users could close any network files or folders they are using. To communicate with network users, the administrator sends a "console message" that appears in a dialog box on each user's computer.

These messages are sent using a service called Messenger, but do not confuse this with the Windows Messenger or MSN Messenger programs that send instant messages.

Unfortunately, some advertising companies figured out a way to tap into the Messenger service and use it to send ads to Windows computers over the Internet. These ads are virtually untraceable and extremely annoying. Fortunately, you can prevent these ads from appearing by shutting down the Messenger service.

① Click start.

② Click Control Panel.

The Control Panel window appears.

③ Click Performance and Maintenance.

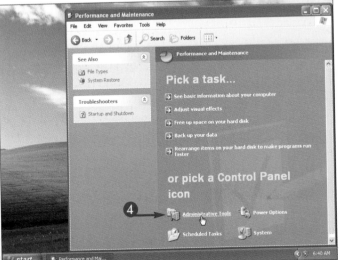

The Performance and Maintenance window appears.

④ Click Administrative Tools.

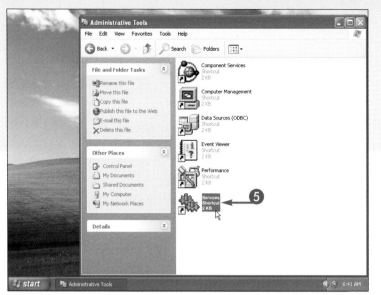

The Administrative Tools window appears.

⑤ Double-click Services.

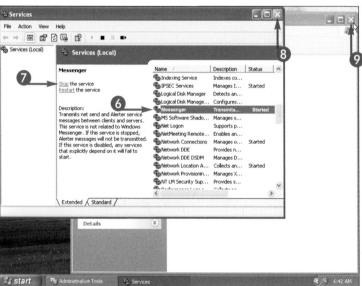

The Services window appears.

⑥ Click the Messenger service.

⑦ Click Stop.

⑧ Click here to close the Services window.

⑨ Click here to close the Administrative Tools window.

Windows shuts down the Messenger service.

 TIPS

More Options!

If you do not see the Stop link, the Messenger service may be disabled, which is the case on most XP systems with Service Pack 2 installed. To make sure the service is disabled, follow Steps **1** to **6** and then click Action and then Properties. In the "Startup type" list, click ⊻ and then click Disabled. Click OK.

Did You Know?

If you want to send console messages to other users on your network and ignore the threat of remote ads appearing, enable and then start the Messenger service. Follow Steps **1** to **4** and then double-click Computer Management. Click Shared Folder and then click Action, All Tasks, and Send Console Message. Type your message in the Message box. Click Add, enter the network computer name, click OK, and repeat as necessary. Click Send to deliver the message.

Guard your
INTERNET PASSWORDS

You can keep your Internet passwords safe by forcing Internet Explorer not to save them on your computer.

Many World Wide Web sites require registration to access certain pages and content. In almost all cases, before you can navigate to any of these restricted pages you must first enter a password, along with your user name or e-mail address. When you fill in this information and log on to the site, Internet Explorer displays the AutoComplete dialog box and offers to remember the password so that you do not have to type it again when you visit the same page in

the future. If you click Yes and then access the site at a later date, Internet Explorer bypasses the login page and takes you directly to the site.

This is convenient, to be sure, but it has a downside: Anyone who uses your computer can also access the password-protected content. If you do not want this to happen, one solution is to click No when Internet Explorer asks to remember the password. Alternatively, you can tell Internet Explorer not to remember any passwords, as described in this task.

❶ Click start.

❷ Right-click Internet.

❸ Click Internet Properties.

Note: If Internet Explorer is running, you can also click Tools and then Internet Options.

The Internet Properties dialog box appears.

❹ Click the Content tab.

❺ Click AutoComplete.

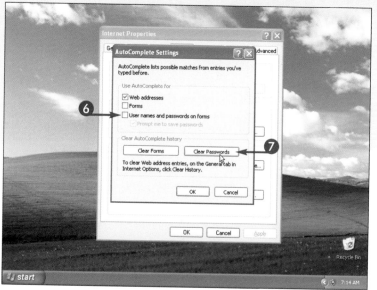

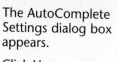

The AutoComplete Settings dialog box appears.

#50

DIFFICULTY LEVEL

⑥ Click User names and passwords on forms (☑ changes to ☐).

⑦ Click Clear Passwords.

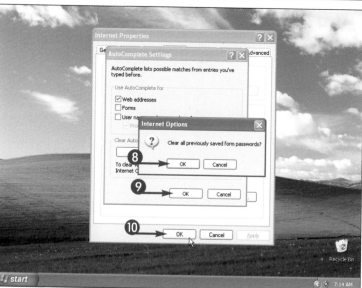

The Internet Options dialog box appears.

⑧ Click OK to return to the AutoComplete Settings dialog box.

⑨ Click OK to return to the Internet Properties dialog box.

⑩ Click OK.

Windows disables the AutoComplete feature.

TIPS

Important!

Many Web sites offer to "remember" your login information. They do this by placing your user name and password in a small file called a *cookie* that gets stored on your computer. Although safe, it may lead to a problem: Other people who use your computer can access the password-protected content. To avoid this, be sure to click the check box that asks if you want to save your login data (☑ changes to ☐).

Did You Know?

If you already have some login cookies stored on your computer, you may want to delete them. To do this, follow Steps **1** to **3**, click the General tab, and then click Delete Cookies. In the Delete Cookies dialog box, click OK.

RESTRICT
Internet content

You can restrict Internet content to prevent children and other unauthorized users from viewing sites that display inappropriate language, nudity, sex, or violence.

The World Wide Web is a vast information source, much of which is helpful or educational or, at worst, innocuous. However, no central authority or government directs the Web, which means that controlling what gets put on the Web is nearly impossible. As a result, many sites display content that is unsuitable for children, or that is otherwise objectionable to some viewers. Profanity, nudity, sex, and violence are all on the Web, sometimes in extreme form.

If you have children who access the Web, if you want to avoid objectionable content yourself, or if you run an office and do not want employees viewing obscene materials, Internet Explorer can help. The Content Advisor feature enables you to set up ratings that determine the maximum acceptable level of content in four categories: language, nudity, sex, and violence. To view any site that displays content beyond these ratings, the user must enter a "supervisor" password.

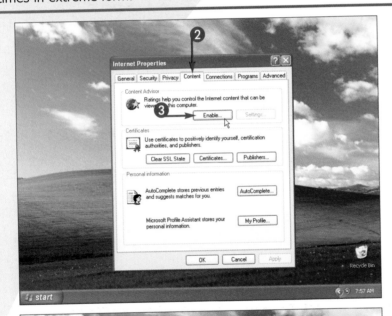

① Follow Steps **1** to **3** in Task #50 to display the Internet Properties dialog box.

② Click the Content tab.

③ Click Enable.

The Content Advisor dialog box appears.

④ Click a category.

⑤ Click and drag the slider to set the maximum rating that unauthorized users can see.

⑥ Repeat Steps **4** to **5** for each category with which you want to work.

⑦ Click OK.

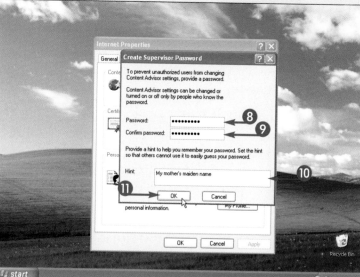

The Create Supervisor Password dialog box appears.

⑧ Type the password.

⑨ Retype the password.

⑩ Type a hint for the password.

⑪ Click OK.

DIFFICULTY LEVEL

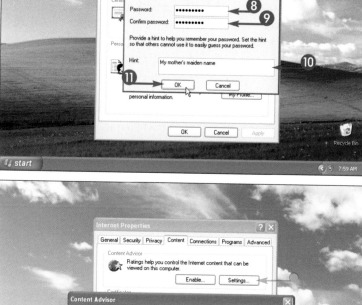

The Content Advisor dialog box appears.

⑫ Click OK to return to the Internet Properties dialog box.

● To make changes to the Content Advisor ratings in the future, you can click Settings, type your supervisor password, and click OK.

⑬ Click OK.

Windows restricts Internet content.

TIPS

More Options!

You can also restrict Web content by site. For example, if you know of a site that you never want unauthorized users to view, regardless of the page ratings, you can specify that site's address as "never viewable." In the Content Advisor dialog box, click the Approved Sites tab, type the site address, and then click Never.

More Options!

You can change your supervisor password. In the Content Advisor dialog box, click the General tab and then click Change Password. Type your old password, type your new password, confirm your new password, type a password hint, and then click OK.

Set the Web
SECURITY LEVEL

You can specify a different security level to make your Web surfing sessions safer.

Web pages can contain small programs, scripts, and other so-called *active* content. This active content is designed to offer you a more lively and interactive experience. However, dangers are associated with such content, just as with any remote program that runs on your computer. For example, some scripts can access the data on your hard drive. Fortunately, the vast majority of sites that use such content do so

responsibly and safely. However, there are ways to use such content for nefarious purposes, and many Web pages are set up to do just that.

Therefore, it pays to be always vigilant when you are on the Web. You can do this by setting the appropriate security level for the Web "zone." The security level determines what types of active content can run, either with or without your permission. The higher the level, the less active content that can run, although the less interesting and interactive your Web sessions will be.

① Click start.

② Right-click Internet.

③ Click Internet Properties.

> *Note: If Internet Explorer is running, you can also click Tools and then Internet Options.*

The Internet Properties dialog box appears.

④ Click the Security tab.

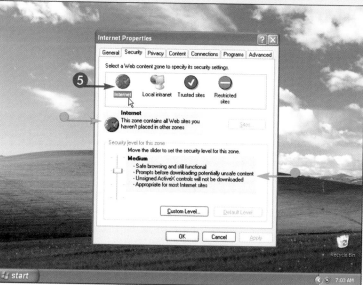

⑤ Click Internet.

● This area describes the current zone.

● This area describes the current security level for the zone.

⑥ Click and drag the Security level slider to the level you want.

Note: If the current security level is listed as Custom, click Default Level. This sets the security level for the Internet to Medium, which is a good choice for most people.

⑦ Click OK.

Windows changes the Web security level.

TIPS

More Options!

Internet Explorer has a "Trusted sites" zone that uses the Low security level. This level is easier to use because you see fewer warnings and more types of content appear on the page. However, safety is also minimal, so use it only for Web sites that you trust completely. To add a site to this zone, click Trusted sites, click Sites, type the address, and click Add.

More Options!

If other people use your computer, you may want to prevent them from downloading any files from the Web. To do this, click Custom Level in the Internet Properties dialog box to display the Security Settings dialog box. In the Settings list, scroll down to the File download option, and then click Disable (○ changes to ⦿). Click OK.

THWART E-MAIL VIRUSES #53
by reading messages in text

You can reduce the danger of accidentally unleashing a virus on your computer by reading all your e-mail messages in text format.

E-mail messages come in two formats: plain text and HTML. The HTML format utilizes the same codes that are used to create Web pages. Therefore, just as some Web pages are unsafe, so are some e-mail messages. Specifically, messages can contain scripts that run automatically when you open or even just preview a message. You can prevent these scripts from running by viewing all your messages in the plain text format.

TIP

Did You Know?
When you are viewing a message as plain text, you may realize that the message is innocuous and that it is okay to view the HTML version. To switch quickly to HTML, click View and then click Message in HTML. You can also press Alt+Shift+H.

① In Outlook Express, click Tools.

Note: If you do not have Outlook Express running, click start and then E-mail.

② Click Options.

The Options dialog box appears.

③ Click the Read tab.

④ Click Read all messages in plain text (☐ changes to ☑).

⑤ Click OK.

E-mail messages now appear only in plain text.

THWART WEB BUGS
by blocking images in messages

You can make your e-mail address more private by thwarting the Web bugs that are inserted into some e-mail messages.

A *Web bug* is a small and usually invisible image, the code for which is inserted into an e-mail message. That code specifies a remote address from which to download the Web bug image when you open or preview the message. However, the code also includes a reference to your e-mail address. The remote server makes note of the fact that you received the message, which means your address is a working one and is therefore a good target for further spam messages. By blocking Web bugs, you undermine this confirmation and so receive less spam.

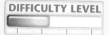

TIP

Did You Know?
To see the images in a legitimate e-mail message, click View and then click Blocked Images. Alternatively, in the preview pane, click "Click here to download pictures."

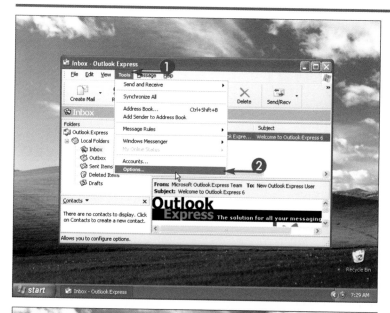

1. In Outlook Express, click Tools.

   Note: If you do not have Outlook Express running, click start and then E-mail.

2. Click Options.

The Options dialog box appears.

3. Click the Security tab.

4. Click Block images and other external content in HTML e-mail (☐ changes to ☑).

5. Click OK.

Windows blocks images and other external content in HTML e-mail.

Maximize your
E-MAIL SECURITY

You can set an option in Outlook Express that maximizes the security of your e-mail.

In Task #52, you learned about security levels for the Web, but they also apply to e-mail. The Medium level is suitable for the Web, but your e-mail should use the maximum level, which is High. This is the level used with the Restricted sites zone, and this task shows you how to apply that level to your e-mail.

DIFFICULTY LEVEL

More Options!

While you are in the Security tab, also click "Do not allow attachments to be saved or opened that could potentially be a virus" (☐ changes to ☑) and "Warn me when other applications try to send mail as me" (☐ changes to ☑).

① In Outlook Express, click Tools.

   Note: If you do not have Outlook Express running, click start and then E-mail.

② Click Options.

The Options dialog box appears.

③ Click the Security tab.

④ Click Restricted sites zone (☐ changes to ☑).

⑤ Click OK.

   Outlook changes the e-mail security level.

Prevent Outlook Express from
SENDING A READ RECEIPT

DIFFICULTY LEVEL

You can block Outlook Express from sending a message that confirms you have opened a message.

A *read receipt* is a short message that Outlook Express automatically fires back to the sender when you open or preview a message from that person. The read receipt — which must be requested by the sender — ensures the sender that you have viewed the message. Many people consider this an invasion of privacy, so they block Outlook Express from sending out these read receipts.

TIP

More Options!

You may find that read receipts are useful in business. For example, if someone sends you an important message, it is easier to confirm that you have received the message by having Outlook Express send a read receipt than sending a response yourself. In that case, click "Notify me for each read receipt request" (○ changes to ◉). This enables you to control when you send a read receipt.

1 In Outlook Express, click Tools.

Note: If you do not have Outlook Express running, click start and then E-mail.

2 Click Options.

The Options dialog box appears.

3 Click the Receipts tab.

4 Click Never send a read receipt (○ changes to ◉).

5 Click OK.

Outlooks stops sending read receipts to confirm that you have read e-mail.

BLOCK PEOPLE
whose messages you do not want

You can configure Outlook Express to reject incoming messages that come from a particular address. This enables you to block people who send you annoying or offensive messages.

E-mail is a truly useful tool, and few people would voluntarily do without it for any length of time. But the usefulness of e-mail falls in proportion to the number of useless messages we receive. Spam (unsolicited commercial messages; see Task #58) is a big problem, of course, and is for most people the largest source of their junk messages. However, even

if you get little in the way of spam, you may get annoying or offensive messages from certain people. It could be a relatively harmless "forwarder" who constantly passes along jokes, lists, and other trivia, or a more serious "e-stalker" who hassles you with a barrage of messages. In either case, you can clean up your Inbox and prevent further abuse by blocking the offending person so that Outlook Express rejects any further messages that originate from that person's address.

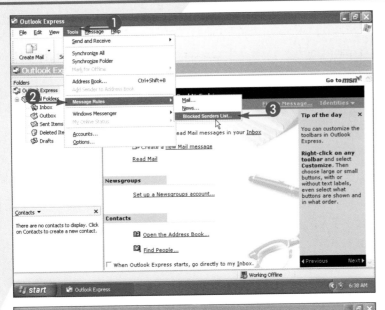

❶ In Outlook Express, click Tools.

❷ Click Message Rules.

❸ Click Blocked Senders List.

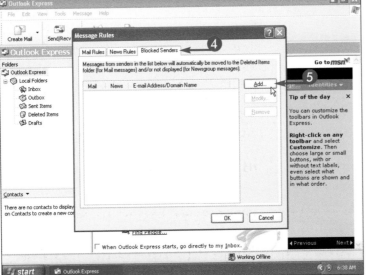

The Message Rules dialog box appears.

❹ Click the Blocked Senders tab.

❺ Click Add.

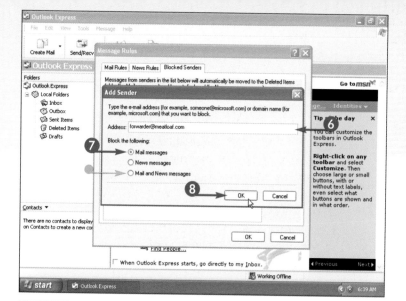

The Add Sender dialog box appears.

⑥ Type the address of the person you want to block.

⑦ Click Mail messages (○ changes to ⊙).

● If you also receive messages from this person via newsgroups, click Mail and News messages instead (○ changes to ⊙).

⑧ Click OK.

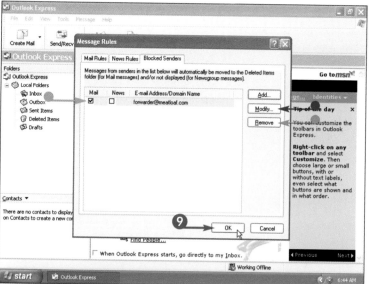

● The person's address appears in the Blocked Senders tab.

● To change the address, you can click the address and then click Modify.

● To stop blocking this person's messages, you can click the address and then click Remove.

⑨ Click OK.

Outlook rejects e-mail from the address you specified.

Did You Know?

If you have an e-mail message from the offending person, there is a quicker way to add him or her to the Blocked Senders list. Click the message and then click Message and then Block Sender. Outlook Express adds the address to the Blocked Senders list and asks if you want to delete all of the person's messages. Click Yes.

More Options!

The *domain* of an address is the part that comes after the @ sign: microsoft.com, whitehouse.gov, and so on. In some cases, you may need to block all messages that come from a particular domain. To do this, type just the domain part of the address in the Add Sender dialog box.

BLOCK SPAM
messages

You can configure Outlook Express to check incoming messages for the presence of certain words that identify the message as spam. Doing this enables you to automatically move such messages to another folder or even to delete them.

If you are like most people, you probably get lots of unsolicited commercial e-mail, more commonly known as *spam*. You may get dozens of such messages a day, although some unlucky people get *hundreds* of spams daily. These annoyances are not only frustrating and time-consuming, but they are often offensive with their come-ons for pornographic

sites and body enhancement products. You can get the upper hand on spam by configuring Outlook Express to look for telltale words and phrases that identify a message as spam. You can then have the program move those messages to a special folder, or have them deleted outright.

You do this by specifying one or more "rules" that Outlook Express applies to each incoming message. For example, you may specify that if a message contains the phrases *maximize your income* or *free trial* in the Subject line, the message is probably spam, so either move or delete it.

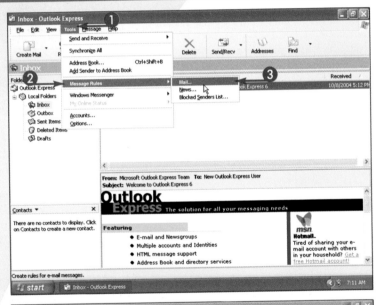

① In Outlook Express, click Tools.

② Click Message Rules.

③ Click Mail.

The New Mail Rule dialog box appears.

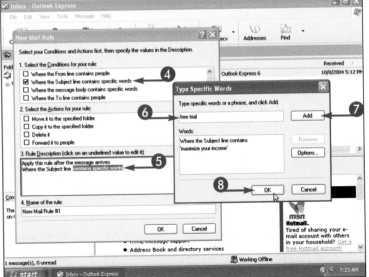

④ Click a condition that you want to apply to test the incoming message (☐ changes to ☑).

⑤ Click the link in the Rule Description box.

⑥ Type the word or phrase.

⑦ Click Add.

Note: Repeat Steps 6 to 7 as necessary.

⑧ Click OK.

Note: You can specify multiple conditions for a rule by repeating Steps 4 to 8.

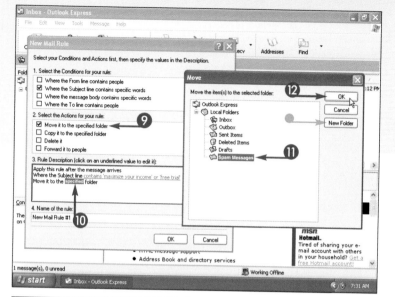

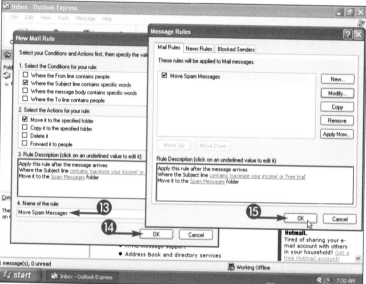

9 Click an action that you want to take for any message that meets your condition (□ changes to ☑).

10 Click the link in the Rule Description box.

11 Click the folder.

● You can click New Folder to create a folder.

12 Click OK.

 # 58

13 Type a name for the rule.

14 Click OK.

The Message Rules dialog box appears.

15 Click OK.

Outlook places spam e-mail in the folder you specified.

TIPS

More Options!

After you create your first rule, clicking the Mail command (Step **3**) takes you directly to the Message Rules dialog box. To create a rule from there, click the Mail Rules tab and then click New.

Did You Know?

Here are some spam-identifying words and phrases to look for in the Subject line or message body: 18+, adult, adv, casino, credit rating, debts, dieting, diploma, double your money, e-mail marketing, erotic, free phone, free trial, free vacation, free!, get out of debt, giveaway, guaranteed!, hair loss, hormone, increase your sales, incredible opportunity, lose weight, maximize your income, millionaire, over 18, over 21, printer cartridge, reach millions, secure your future, sex, thinning hair, too good to be true, urgent notice, Viagra, work at home, XXX, you are a winner.

PASSWORD-PROTECT
your Outlook Express identity

You can create separate identities in Outlook Express to keep e-mail messages for multiple people separated. To ensure privacy, you can apply a password to your identity.

If multiple people use your computer, each person likely has his or her own e-mail address. If so, keeping the e-mail addresses separated to avoid confusion and ensure privacy is important. One way to do this is to create individual accounts in the User Accounts feature of Windows XP.

If creating individual accounts is not feasible or practical on your computer, you can also create a separate Outlook Express identity for each user. An *identity* is a collection of e-mail accounts. When you log on to your identity, you can add or delete accounts and also send and receive messages on those accounts. If someone else then logs on using a different identity, he or she works with a completely different set of accounts and cannot see yours. To ensure the privacy of your identity, you can also apply a logon password.

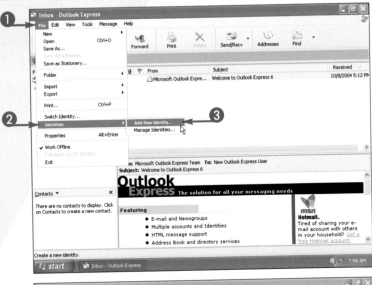

① In Outlook Express, click File.

② Click Identities.

③ Click Add New Identity.

The New Identity dialog box appears.

④ Type a name for your identity.

⑤ Click Require a password
(☐ changes to ☑).

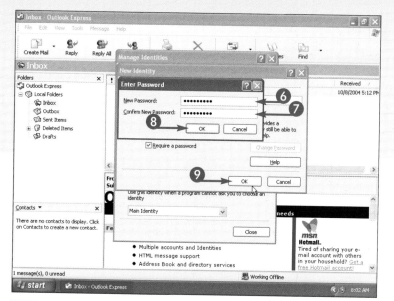

The Enter Password dialog box appears.

6 Type your password.

7 Type your password again.

8 Click OK.

9 Click OK.

The Identity Added dialog box appears.

10 Click Yes.

59

DIFFICULTY LEVEL

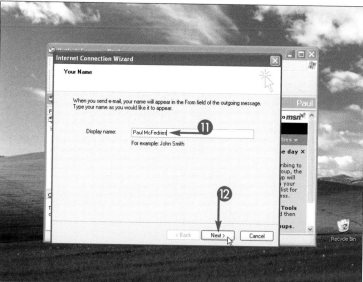

11 In the Internet Connection Wizard, type your name.

12 Click Next.

13 Continue with the wizard to create an account for your new identity.

Note: To complete the wizard, you will need the identity's e-mail address, the address of your ISP's incoming and outgoing mail servers, and the account's user name and password.

Outlook Express password protects the new identity.

More Options!

To log off the current identity and log on to a different one, click File, and then Switch Identity to display the Switch Identities dialog box. Click the identity, type the password, and then click OK.

More Options!

To make changes to the identities, click File, Identities, and Manage Identities to display the Manage Identities dialog box. To change a name or password, click the identity and then click Properties. To delete an identity, click the identity, click Remove, and then click Delete. Type the identity's password and click OK. Note, however, that you cannot delete an identity if it is currently logged on. You must first log off the identity and then delete it.

Play Internet media
SAFELY

DIFFICULTY LEVEL

You can set options in Windows Media Player (WMP) that ensure media downloaded from or played on an Internet site is safe.

You can play Internet media either by downloading the music or video to your computer and playing it in WMP, or by using a version of WMP that resides inside a Web page. Either way, the person who created the media may have included extra commands in a *script* that is designed to control the playback.

Unfortunately, scripts can also contain commands that can harm your computer, so preventing these scripts from running is the best option.

TIP

More Options!

Some media sites display *enhanced content*, or Web pages that give you information related to the media. Because these pages can contain malicious content, WMP asks if you want to see the enhanced content. If you trust your sites, bypass this prompt by clicking "Do not prompt me before playing enhanced content that uses Web pages" (☐ changes to ☑).

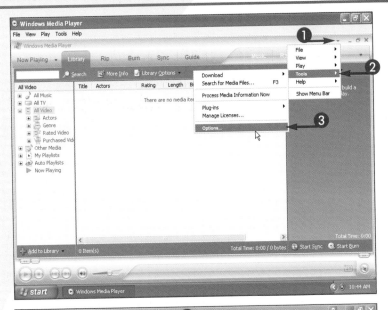

❶ In Windows Media Player, click the Access Application Menus button.

❷ Click Tools.

❸ Click Options.

❹ In the Options dialog box, click the Security tab.

❺ Click here to avoid downloading and running scripts on your computer (☑ changes to ☐).

❻ Click here to avoid running scripts for Web page media (☑ changes to ☐).

❼ Click OK.

Windows Media Player applies the new security settings to the Internet media you play.

Play Internet media
PRIVATELY

You can set options in Windows Media Player (WMP) that enhance the privacy of the Internet media you play.

When you use WMP to play content from an Internet site, WMP communicates certain information to the site, including the unique ID number of your copy of WMP. This allows content providers to track the media you play, and they may share this data with other sites. So although the Player ID does not identify you personally, it may result in sites sending you targeted ads based on your media choices. If you do not want such an invasion of privacy, you can instruct WMP not to send the Player ID.

Important!

Remember that some content sites *require* the Player ID before you can play any media. For example, a site may request the ID for billing purposes. In that case, you should read the site's privacy statement to see what uses it makes of the ID.

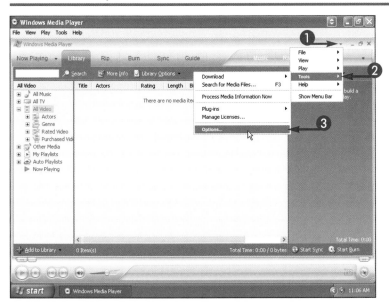

① Click the Access Application Menus button.

② Click Tools.

③ Click Options.

The Options dialog box appears.

④ Click the Privacy tab.

⑤ Click here to avoid sending your Player ID to content sites (☐ changes to ☑).

⑥ Click here to avoid sharing your WMP usage data with Microsoft (☐ changes to ☑).

⑦ Click here to avoid storing your media filenames and Internet addresses (☑ changes to ☐).

⑧ Click OK.

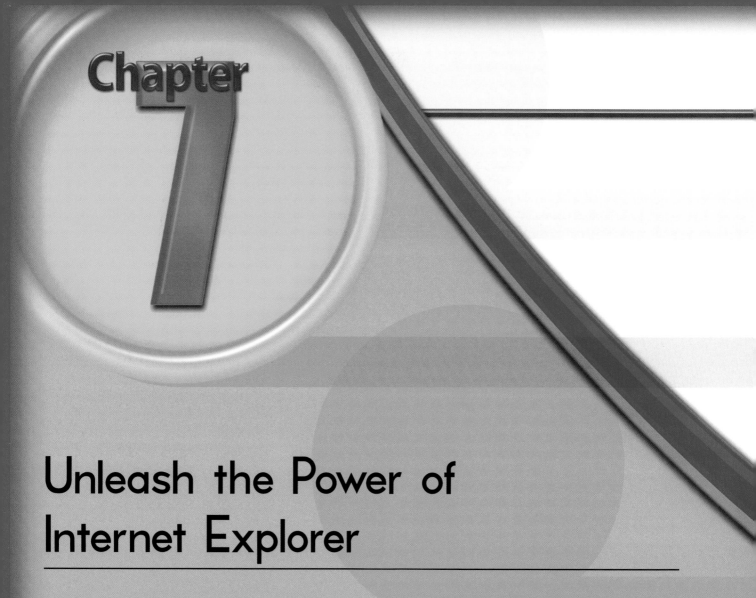

Chapter
1

Unleash the Power of Internet Explorer

The World Wide Web is arguably the most impressive of the various services accessible via the Internet. With *billions* of pages available covering practically every imaginable topic, the Web is one of our greatest inventions and an unparalleled source of information.

One problem with the Web, though, is actually getting at all that information. With so much online ground to cover, you want a reliable and efficient means of transportation. For the World Wide Web, the vehicle of choice is the Web browser, and in Windows XP, the default Web browser is Internet Explorer. This program is fairly easy to use if all you do is click links and type Web site addresses. But to get the

most out of the Web, you can tap into the impressive array of features and options that Internet Explorer offers.

This chapter helps you do just that by taking you through a few truly useful tips and tricks that unleash the power of Internet Explorer. You learn how to take full advantage of the Links bar by customizing it for easier and more efficient Web surfing; save copies of Web page images to your computer; turn off those unpleasant and unnecessary Web page sounds and animations; search for Web sites directly from the Internet Explorer Address bar; clear Address bar addresses to maintain the privacy of your surfing; and block those annoying pop-up ads.

Top 100

CUSTOMIZE THE LINKS BAR
for easier surfing

You can customize Internet Explorer's Links bar to provide easy one-click access to those Web sites that you visit most often.

One of Internet Explorer's most useful features is also one of its most hidden. The Links bar is easy to miss, tucked away on the far right of the window beside the Address bar. It consists of a collection of buttons, each of which is associated with a Web site. When you click a button, Internet Explorer automatically navigates to the associated site. This

makes it easy to get to the home pages of Windows XP and Windows Media because those two sites are part of the default Links bar. However, the Links bar is fully customizable. Not only can you move it to a more accessible place in the Internet Explorer window, but you can also populate it with new buttons associated with the sites you visit most often. This task takes you through these and other Links bar customizations.

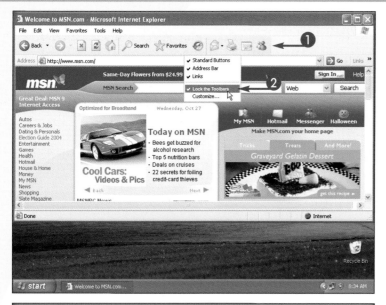

MAKE THE LINKS BAR MORE ACCESSIBLE

1 In Internet Explorer, right-click any toolbar.

2 Click Lock the Toolbars (☑ disappears).

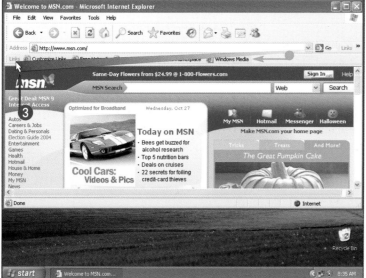

3 Click and drag the Links bar, and drop it below the Address bar.

● The entire Links bar appears.

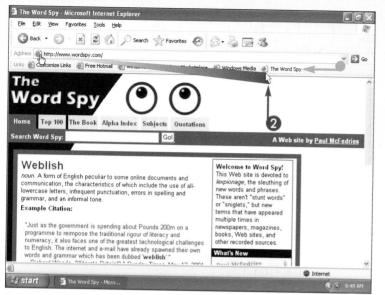

CREATE A BUTTON FOR THE CURRENT WEB PAGE

DIFFICULTY LEVEL

① Navigate to the page with which you want to work.

② Click and drag the Address bar icon and drop it on the Links bar.

● A new button associated with the page appears on the Links bar. You can click this button to navigate directly to the page.

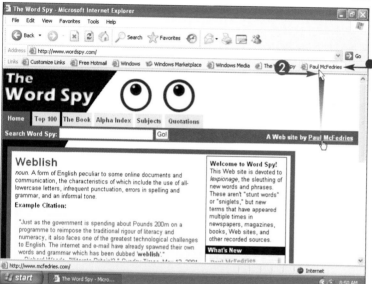

CREATE A BUTTON FROM A WEB PAGE LINK

① Navigate to the page that contains the link with which you want to work.

② Click and drag the link text and drop it on the Links bar.

● A new button associated with the linked page appears on the Links bar. You can click this button to navigate directly to the linked page.

TIPS

Customize It!

The positions of the Links bar buttons are not fixed. To move a button to another position, click and drag the button and then drop it in the position you prefer. To rename a button, right-click it, click Rename, type the new name in the Rename dialog box, and then click OK. To delete a button, right-click it, click Delete, and then click Yes when Windows XP asks you to confirm.

Did You Know?

If the address of one of your sites changes, you can edit the address associated with the site's Links bar button. Right-click the button and then click Properties. In the button's Properties dialog box, type the new address in the URL text box. Click OK.

SAVE AN IMAGE
to your computer

You can save a copy of a Web page image to a folder on your computer, enabling you to use the image for your personal documents. If the image is in the public domain, you can then use the image any way you choose. However, most Web images are the copyright of the Web site owner. You can still copy such images, but your use of them is restricted to personal documents such as greeting cards or posters, your desktop background, or other noncommercial uses.

DIFFICULTY LEVEL

TIP

More Options!

When you right-click a Web page image, the shortcut menu gives you several other options. To send the image to another person via e-mail, click E-mail Picture. To print a copy of the picture, click Print Picture. To use the image as the background image for your Windows XP desktop, click Set as Background.

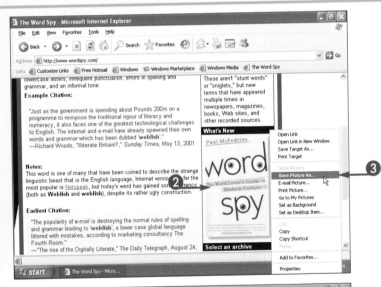

1 In Internet Explorer, navigate to the page that contains the image you want to save.

2 Right-click the image.

3 Click Save Picture As.

The Save Picture dialog box appears.

4 Click here and then click the folder in which you want to save the image. (The default folder is My Pictures.)

5 Type a name for the image.

6 Click here and then click an image type.

7 Click Save.

Windows XP saves the image to your computer.

DIFFICULTY LEVEL

You can configure Internet Explorer to not play Web page sounds and animations.

Most professionally designed Web sites are easy on the eyes and ears. Unfortunately, most Web sites are not professionally designed, and these amateur sites are all too often marred by ugly animations and annoying sounds embedded in their pages. Fortunately, you can configure Internet Explorer to avoid playing this media. Doing so rarely affects the usefulness of any site, and it gives your eyes and ears some peace.

TIP

More Options!

If you have a slow Internet connection, you can speed up your Web surfing by turning off Web page images. Follow Steps **1** to **3** and then click Show pictures (☑ changes to ☐). Internet Explorer will show empty boxes where each image would have been. To view an image, right-click its image box and then click Show Picture.

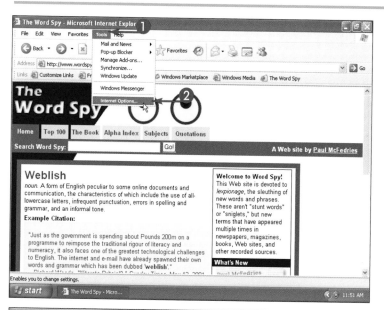

1 In Internet Explorer, click Tools.

2 Click Internet Options.

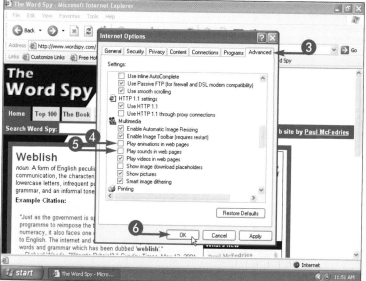

The Internet Options dialog box appears.

3 Click the Advanced tab.

4 Click Play animations in web pages (☑ changes to ☐).

5 Click Play sounds in web pages (☑ changes to ☐).

6 Click OK.

Internet Explorer puts the options into effect.

Search from the
ADDRESS BAR

You can perform World Wide Web searches directly from the Internet Explorer Address bar, which is much faster and more efficient than using the Search Companion.

With billions of pages, the World Wide Web is an amazing information resource. However, it can also be a frustrating resource because *finding* the page you want among those billions is a real challenge. You can ask friends and family, or you can use a site such as yahoo.com that categorizes pages, but these strategies are often unreliable.

To find the site you want, you can take advantage of the various search engines that enable you to find Web pages based on the search text you provide. Internet Explorer's Search Companion (click the Search button in the toolbar) uses the MSN Search site to perform its searches. However, using the Search Companion takes a few steps, and you must contend with the animated dog that few people like.

Fortunately, you can bypass the Search Companion and perform searches directly from the Internet Explorer Address bar. As you see in this task, this method is the faster and more efficient way to search the Web.

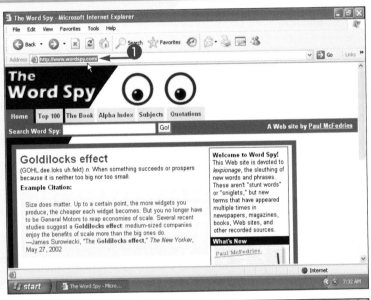

① In Internet Explorer, click the Address bar to select the current address.

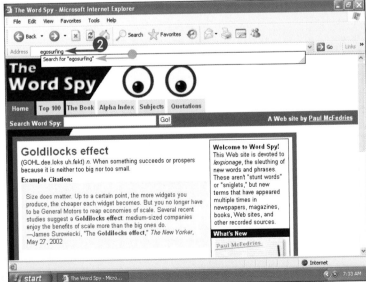

② Type the word or phrase for which you want to search.

● As you type, Internet Explorer displays "Search for" followed by your typed words.

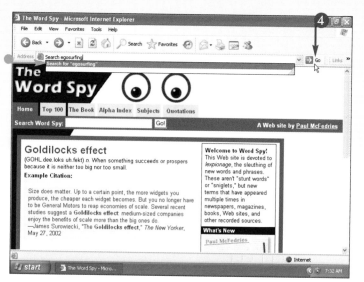

3 Press the Tab key.

● Internet Explorer selects the "Search for" text.

4 Click Go (or press the Enter key).

 # 65

DIFFICULTY LEVEL

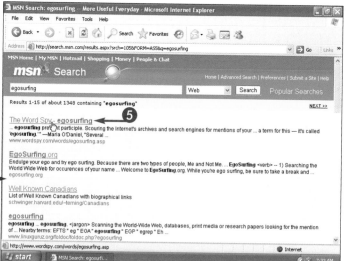

● Internet Explorer displays the search results.

5 Click a site that appears to satisfy your search.

TIPS

Did You Know?

You can perform Address bar searching without having to select the "Search for" text. In the Address bar, before you type your search text, type **?**, **go**, **find**, or **search**, type a space, type your search text, and then press the Enter key.

Check This Out!

If you love the Google search engine, you can install the Google toolbar, which becomes part of the Internet Explorer window. You can then perform Google searches directly from the toolbar, which also gives you quick access to other Google features. For more information and to download the Google toolbar, go to http://toolbar.google.com.

SET UP ANOTHER SEARCH ENGINE
for Address bar searching

You can customize Address bar searching to use a search engine other than the default MSN Search, enabling you to use your favorite search engine directly from the Address bar.

If you have used the World Wide Web for a while, then you have probably noticed that not all search sites are created equal. Some search engines just seem to provide results that are consistently more reliable and targeted than other search engines. That is not surprising because search sites index the Web differently and use different searching programs.

If you have a search engine other than MSN Search that you prefer above all others, you may decide that it is worth the extra effort to navigate to that site rather than using MSN Search via the Internet Explorer Address bar. However, you can have it both ways. As you see in this task, you can configure Internet Explorer to use your favorite search engine to perform your Address bar searching chores.

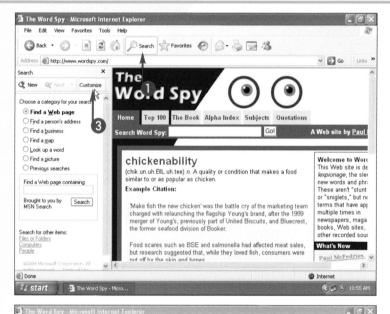

① In Internet Explorer, click Search.

② Switch to the classic Search layout, as described in the tip on the following page.

③ Click Customize.

The Customize Search Settings dialog box appears.

④ Click Autosearch settings.

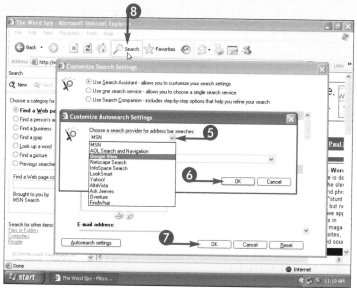

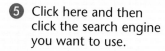

The Customize
Autosearch Settings
dialog box appears.

⑤ Click here and then
click the search engine
you want to use.

⑥ Click OK to return to
the Customize Search
Settings dialog box.

⑦ Click OK.

⑧ Click Search to close
the Search bar.

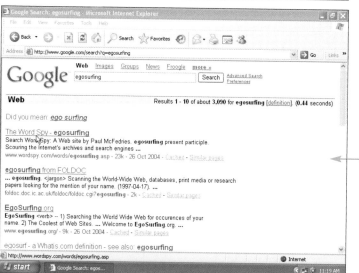

● When you run a search from the Address
bar, Internet Explorer now uses the search
engine you chose in Step **5**.

Customize It!

You can customize the Search Companion
to use a search engine other than MSN
Search. In the toolbar, click Search, click
"Change preferences," and then click
"Change Internet search behavior." In the
"Select the default search engine" list, click
the search engine you want to use and
then click OK.

Did You Know?

If you want to use the Internet Explorer
Search bar, but you do not like the Search
Companion, you can switch to the classic
Search layout. In the toolbar, click Search,
click "Change preferences," and then click
"Change Internet search behavior." Click
"With Classic Internet search" (○ changes
to ⊙), and then click OK. Shut down and
restart Internet Explorer to put the change
into effect.

REMOVE SAVED ADDRESSES
from the Address bar

You can remove all the addresses that appear in the Internet Explorer Address bar drop-down list, preventing another user of your computer from seeing and visiting those addresses.

You normally use the Internet Explorer Address bar as a text box: You type the Web address you want to visit and then click Go or press the Enter key. But the Address bar also doubles as a drop-down list. Click the Address bar drop-down list and you see a list of the last few addresses that you have typed into the Address bar text box.

This is a useful feature because it enables you to revisit a site simply by dropping down the list and clicking the site address. However, it is also a dangerous feature if other people use your computer. Those users can just as easily visit those addresses, which could be a problem if the address points to a financial site, private corporate site, or some other page that you would not want another person to visit. Fortunately, you can clear the Address bar list at the end of your surfing sessions.

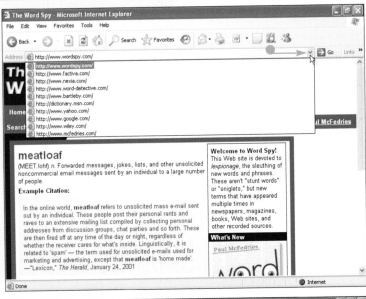

● You can click here to see how many addresses appear in the Internet Explorer Address bar list.

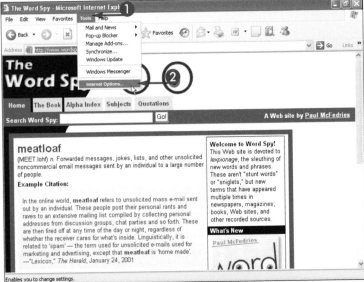

① In Internet Explorer, click Tools.

② Click Internet Options.

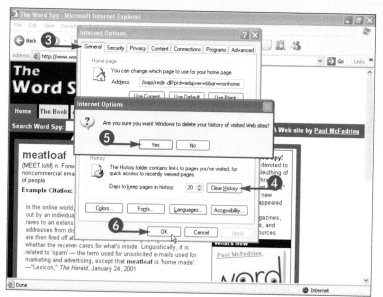

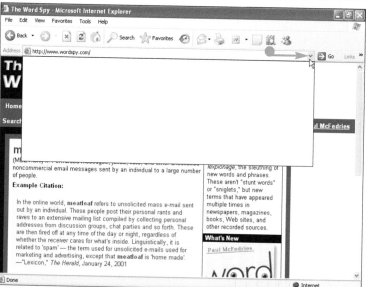

The Internet Options dialog box appears.

③ Click the General tab.

④ Click Clear History.

Internet Explorer asks you to confirm.

⑤ Click Yes to return to the Internet Options dialog box.

Internet Explorer clears the addresses from the Address bar.

⑥ Click OK to close the Internet Options dialog box.

● You can click here to see that no addresses appear in the Internet Explorer Address bar list.

TIPS

Did You Know?

When you click Clear History in the Internet Options dialog box, you also delete Internet Explorer's record of all the pages you have visited over the past 20 days. (Click the toolbar's History button to see this list.) You can configure Internet Explorer to not record *any* of the pages you visit. Follow Steps **1** to **3** to display the General tab of the Internet Options dialog box. Click the "Days to keep pages in history" text box and change the value to 0. Click OK to close the dialog box.

Customize It!

You can also enter Web addresses from the Windows XP taskbar. Right-click an empty section of the taskbar. If you see ☑ beside Lock the Taskbar, click that command. Right-click the taskbar again, click Toolbars, and then click Address. Click and drag the Address label to the left to see the Address bar.

Block
POP-UP ADS

You can improve your surfing experience by configuring Internet Explorer to block World Wide Web advertisements that pop up in small windows when you visit certain sites.

Web page advertising is a necessary evil because Webmasters often need the money from advertisers to help defray the inevitable costs of maintaining a site. Banner ads are a popular choice, but to make more of an impact, advertisers often insist that their ads appear in separate pop-up windows. These pop-ups are everywhere on the Web these days. Small

personal pages may display a single pop-up when you enter or leave the site; some commercial sites displays a few pop-ups as you peruse their pages; and then there are those sites that throw out a barrage of pop-ups. Depending on your level of tolerance, pop-ups are either mildly irritating or downright annoying. Either way, pop-up ads can make surfing the Web a real chore.

Fortunately, the version of Internet Explorer that comes with Windows XP Service Pack 2 has a feature that can block pop-up ads.

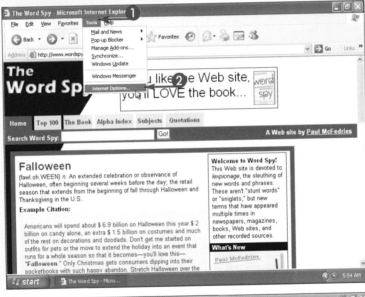

① In Internet Explorer, click Tools.

② Click Internet Options.

The Internet Options dialog box appears.

③ Click the Privacy tab.

④ Click Block pop-ups (☐ changes to ☑).

⑤ Click Settings.

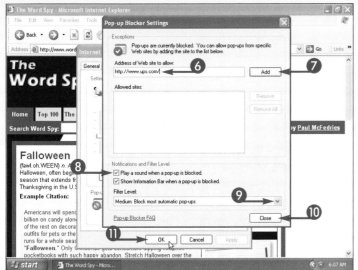

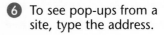

The Pop-up Blocker Settings dialog box appears.

6 To see pop-ups from a site, type the address.

7 Click Add.

8 Click this option to avoid hearing a sound each time a pop-up is blocked (☑ changes to ☐).

9 Click here and then click a blocking level.

10 Click Close.

11 Click OK.

68

DIFFICULTY LEVEL

WORK WITH THE POP-UP BLOCKER

The Information Bar dialog box appears when Internet Explorer blocks a pop-up.

1 Click Do not show this message again (☐ changes to ☑).

2 Click OK.

● The Information Bar appears when Internet Explorer blocks a pop-up. You can click this bar to see the pop-up.

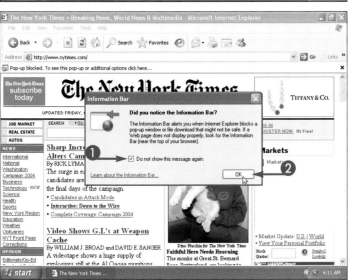

TIPS

More Options!

Some sites display useful information in pop-up windows, and Internet Explorer may block these windows. If so, add the site's address to the list of sites that are allowed to display pop-ups. Navigate to the site and then click Tools, Pop-up Blocker, and then Always Allow Pop-ups from This Site. Click Yes when Internet Explorer asks you to confirm.

Did You Know?

If your version of Internet Explorer does not include the pop-up blocker, there are other tools available that you can use. For example, the Google toolbar described in Task #65 blocks pop-ups, as does the Yahoo! toolbar available here: http://toolbar.yahoo.com/

Chapter 8

Make E-mail Easier

The World Wide Web may be the most impressive of the Internet services, but it would not be hard to make the case that e-mail is the most indispensable. E-mail, which most of us have been using for only a few years, leaves us wondering how we ever managed without it. E-mail's position midway between conversation and letter writing makes it ideal for certain types of communication, and rarely can a person be found nowadays who does not rely on it.

The fact that e-mail is easy to use also helps. Even novice computer users seem to grasp the basic e-mail idea quickly and are often sending messages within minutes. But if, like most people, you use e-mail all day long, you probably want to make it even easier. This

chapter shows you how to do that. The tasks you learn here are designed to save precious seconds and minutes of everyday e-mail chores. That may not sound like much, but added up over the course of a busy e-mail day, those seconds can make the difference between leaving work on time and staying late.

Among the timesavers in this chapter, you learn how to open Outlook Express directly in your Inbox; how to configure Outlook Express to automatically check for messages more often; how to change your message priority; how to create an e-mail distribution list; how to archive your old messages; how to create a backup copy of your address book; and how to exchange electronic business cards.

Top 100

Go to your inbox
AUTOMATICALLY

DIFFICULTY LEVEL

You can configure Outlook Express to automatically display your Inbox. This saves you a step when you start the program.

By default, starting Outlook Express displays the main Outlook Express folder, which tells you how many unread messages you have and offers links to common tasks. However, most people just go immediately to the Inbox folder and work from there. To save this extra step each time you launch Outlook Express, you can configure the program to automatically display the Inbox folder.

Did You Know?
If you start Outlook Express without first connecting to the Internet, the program prompts you to connect so that it can check for new messages. If you would rather work offline at startup, click Tools, Options and then the General tab. Click "Send and receive messages at startup" (☑ changes to ☐) and then click OK.

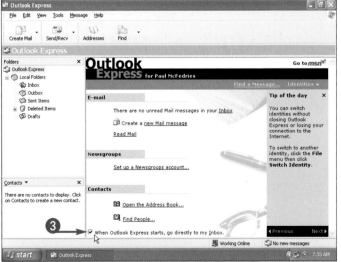

① Click start.

② Click E-mail.

Note: If your Start menu E-mail icon launches a program other than Outlook Express, click start, All Programs, and then Outlook Express.

The Outlook Express window appears.

③ Click When Outlook Express starts, go directly to my Inbox (☐ changes to ☑).

The next time you start Outlook Express, the program displays your Inbox folder automatically.

Change how often you
CHECK FOR MESSAGES

After you start Outlook Express, the program contacts your mail server every 30 minutes to see if any new messages have arrived. You can change the frequency with which Outlook Express checks for new messages to any time between 1 minute and 480 minutes. For example, you may prefer a shorter time if you are expecting an important message. Alternatively, if you want to minimize your connection time, you may prefer a much longer frequency.

More Options!

If you set your e-mail frequency to a value higher than the connection idle time setting (see Task #46), your Internet connection may be disconnected when Outlook Express tries to check for new messages. To work around this problem, follow Steps **1** to **3** and then click ☑ in the "If my computer is not connected at this time" list. Click "Connect only when not working offline" and then click OK.

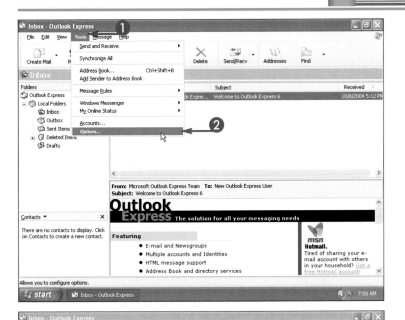

① In Outlook Express, click Tools.

② Click Options.

The Options dialog box appears.

③ Click the General tab.

④ Click Check for new messages every (☐ changes to ☑).

⑤ Type the frequency, in minutes, with which you want to check for messages.

⑥ Click OK.

Outlook Express puts the new setting into effect.

LEAVE YOUR MESSAGES
on the server

You can configure Outlook Express to leave your messages on the server, enabling you to retrieve a message multiple times from different computers.

When you ask Outlook Express to retrieve your messages, it contacts your Internet service provider's e-mail server, downloads the messages, and then deletes them from the server. However, there may be times when you do not want the messages deleted. For example, if you are working at home or on the road and want to retrieve your work messages, it is better to leave them on the server so that you can also retrieve them when you return to the office.

More Options!

Most ISPs offer a limited amount of e-mail storage space, so you cannot leave messages on the server indefinitely. To ensure that your messages are deleted eventually, follow Steps **1** to **6** and then click "Remove from server after *x* days" (☐ changes to ☑), where *x* is the number of days after which you want the server messages deleted.

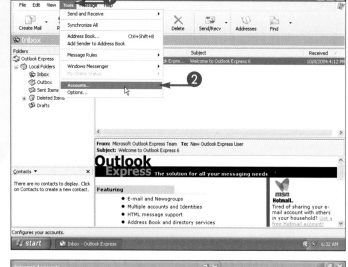

❶ In Outlook Express, click Tools.

❷ Click Accounts.

The Internet Accounts dialog box appears.

❸ Click the account with which you want to work.

❹ Click Properties.

❺ In the account's Properties dialog box, click the Advanced tab.

❻ Click Leave a copy of messages on server (☐ changes to ☑).

❼ Click OK.

❽ Click Close.

Outlook Express leaves a copy of the messages on the server.

You can set the priority level of your outgoing message to let the recipient know whether your message can be handled with high or low priority.

If you are sending a message that has important information or that requires a fast response, set the message's priority to high. When the recipient receives the message, his or her e-mail program will indicate the high priority. For example, Outlook Express indicates high priority messages with a red exclamation mark. Alternatively, you can set the priority to low for unimportant messages so that the recipient knows not to handle the message immediately. Outlook Express flags low priority messages with a blue, downward-pointing arrow.

TIP

Did You Know?

If you are sending important information via e-mail, adding a digital signature to your message ensures the recipient that the message came from you. To get a digital ID, click Tools, Options, the Security tab, and then Get Digital ID. Follow the links in the Web pages that appear. Note that digital IDs cost about $20 per year. To add your digital signature to a message, click Tools and then Digitally Sign.

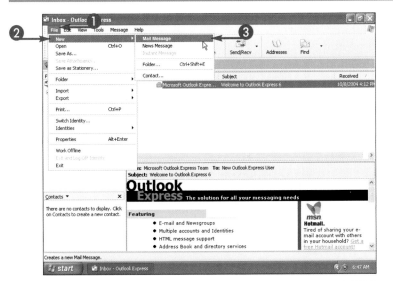

① In Outlook Express, click File.

② Click New.

③ Click Mail Message.

The New Message window appears.

④ Click Message.

⑤ Click Set Priority.

⑥ Click the priority you want to use.

● You can also click Priority in the toolbar.

● When you choose High or Low priority, Outlook Express indicates the current priority level.

Create an
E-MAIL DISTRIBUTION LIST

If you regularly send messages to a particular collection of people, you can organize those recipients into a group. This saves time because when you choose the group as the message recipient, Outlook Express sends the message to every address in the group.

Sending a message to a number of people takes time, because you have to either type many addresses or select many people from your address book. If you find that you are sending some of your

messages to the same group repeatedly, you can avoid the drudgery of adding those recipients individually by creating a *distribution list* or, as Outlook Express calls it, a *group*. After you add the recipients to the list, all you have to do is send the message to the group. Outlook Express then distributes copies of the message to every member of the group. An added benefit is that recipients do not see the names or addresses of the other group members, so maintaining group privacy is easy.

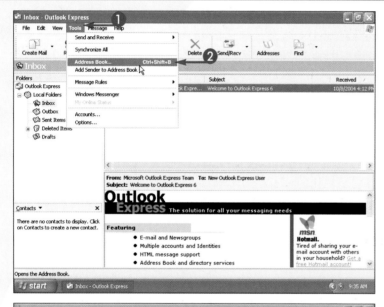

① In Outlook Express, click Tools.

② Click Address Book.

You can also click the Addresses toolbar button, or press Ctrl+Shift+B.

The Address Book window appears.

③ Click File.

④ Click New Group.

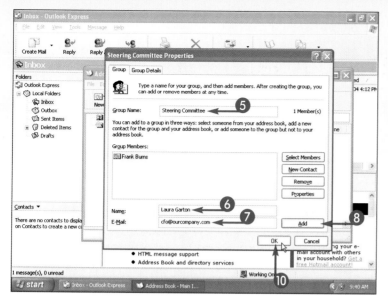

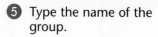
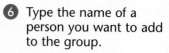

The group's Properties dialog box appears.

5 Type the name of the group.

6 Type the name of a person you want to add to the group.

7 Type the person's e-mail address.

8 Click Add.

9 Repeat Steps **6** to **8** to add other members of the group.

10 Click OK.

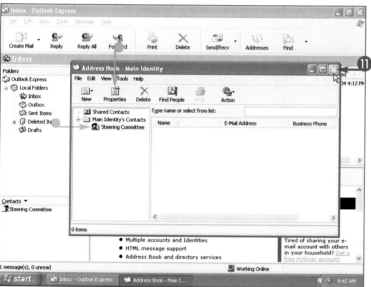

● The group name appears in the Address Book window.

11 Click here to close the Address Book window.

● To make changes to the group, click the group and then click Properties.

TIPS

More Options!
If some or all of the people you want to add to the group are already listed in your Contacts list, you can use an easier method to add them to the group. In the group's Properties dialog box, click Select Members to open the Select Group Members dialog box. Click each person's name you want to add and then click Select. Click OK when you are done.

More Options!
You can add a person to your group *and* add him or her to your Contacts list at the same time. In the group's Properties dialog box, click New Contact. Type the person's name and e-mail address and then click OK. Outlook Express adds the person to your group and to your Contacts list.

You can change the hard drive location that Outlook Express uses to store the contents of your message folders. This is useful if you are running out of space on the current hard drive and need to move the messages to a disk with more free space.

Outlook Express stores the contents of your Inbox, Outbox, Sent Items, Deleted Items, and Drafts folders, as well as any new folders you create, in a special hard drive location called the *message store*. The size of the message store depends on a number

of factors, including how often you use e-mail, how many messages you save, how often you clean out your Deleted Items folder, and so on. However, it is not unusual for the message store to consume dozens or even hundreds of megabytes of disk space. If you are running low on disk space and your computer has another hard drive with more free space, you can give your message store room to grow by moving it to the other disk.

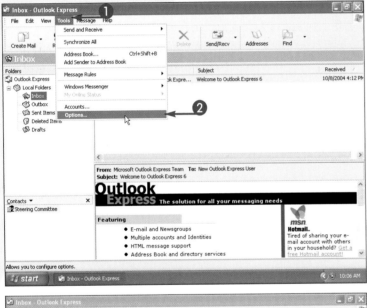

❶ In Outlook Express, click Tools.

❷ Click Options.

The Options dialog box appears.

❸ Click the Maintenance tab.

❹ Click Store Folder.

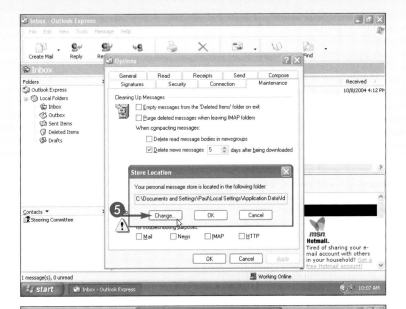

The Store Location dialog box appears.

⑤ Click Change.

The Browse for Folder dialog box appears.

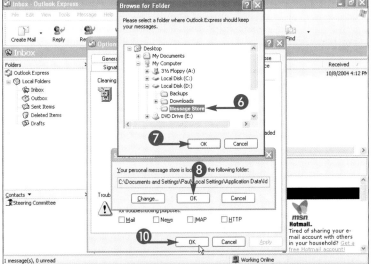

⑥ Click the folder you want to use as the new location.

⑦ Click OK.

⑧ Click OK.

Outlook Express tells you to restart the program to put the new store location into effect.

⑨ Click OK.

⑩ Click OK.

⑪ Shut down and then restart Outlook Express.

Outlook Express moves the message store.

TIPS

Important!
To speed up the process of moving the message store, you can do some folder maintenance before performing these steps. For example, delete any messages you no longer want, including any messages in the Deleted Items folder. You can also delete any folders that you no longer use.

More Options!
Another way to save disk space with Outlook Express is to compact your folders to remove wasted space caused by message deletions. Click File, Folder, and then Compact All Folders.

ARCHIVE
your old messages

You can archive your old messages by saving them outside of Outlook Express. This reduces the disk space used by Outlook Express and makes finding more recent messages easier.

Although you can always delete messages you no longer want, you will still find that you accumulate hundreds, even thousands of messages over the years. Keeping the messages is useful if you ever want to refer to an old message to clarify something. However, the older the message, the less likely it is that you will ever have to refer to it again.

Unfortunately, these old messages take up disk space in the Outlook Express message store (see Task #74) and slow down your message searches. You can overcome both problems by archiving those old messages. In this case, "archiving" means moving the old messages to a separate Outlook Express folder and then copying that folder's corresponding message store file to a new location.

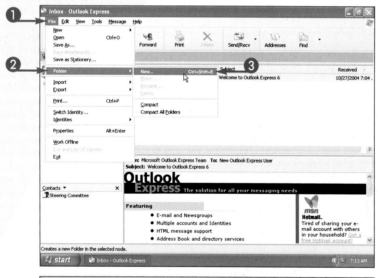

CREATE A FOLDER FOR OLD MESSAGES

① Click File.

② Click Folder.

③ Click New.

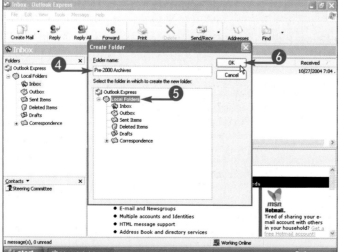

The Create Folder dialog box appears.

④ Type the folder name.

⑤ Click Local Folders.

⑥ Click OK.

Outlook Express adds the folder to the Folders list.

160

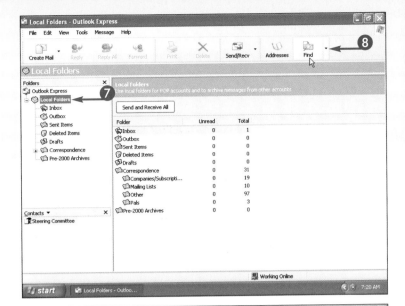

7 Click Local Folders.

8 Click Find.

75

DIFFICULTY LEVEL

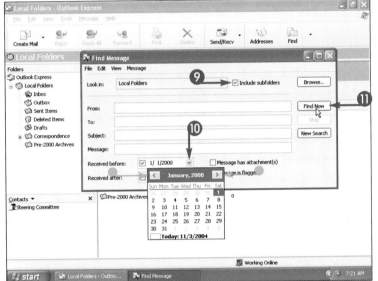

The Find Message dialog box appears.

9 Click Include subfolders (☐ changes to ☑).

10 Click here and click the date before which any messages you received will be archived.

● You can click the arrows to move through the months.

11 Click Find Now.

Try This!

You may prefer to store the messages you have sent in a separate archive. To do that, click the Sent Items folder in Step **7**.

Caution!

If you do not clean out your Deleted Items folder regularly, your search for old messages to archive will also include messages in Deleted Items. To avoid this, you can rearrange your folders a bit. Specifically, move any folders that you have created to store your received messages into the Inbox folder. Then, in Step **7**, click the Inbox folder. Note that your archive will not include the Sent Items folder, so you must create a second archive, as described in the previous tip.

ARCHIVE
your old messages

You can store your archived messages on another hard drive or on a removable disk for safekeeping.

If you are archiving old messages to cut down on the disk space used by the Outlook Express message store, you have a couple of options. First, store the archived messages on a separate hard drive, particularly one that has lots of free space. If you do not have another hard drive, or if you want to store the messages in an off-site location, place the

archive on a removable disk. Chances are the file will be quite large, however, so consider using something other than a floppy disk. Instead, use a Zip disk, flash drive, recordable CD, or some other medium that is large enough to store the archive.

If you must resort to floppy disks, use the Windows XP Backup program to back up the archive. The Backup program splits the archive among multiple floppy disks.

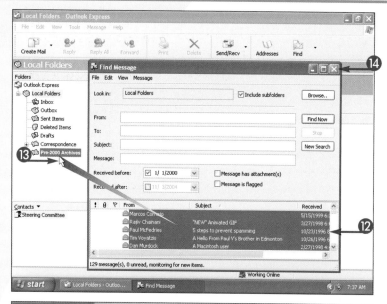

Outlook Express displays a list of messages that you received prior to the date you chose in Step **10**.

⑫ Press Ctrl+A to select all messages.

You can also click a message to select it.

⑬ Click and drag the messages from the Find Message dialog box and drop them on the new folder you created in Steps **1** to **6**.

⑭ Click here to close the Find Message window.

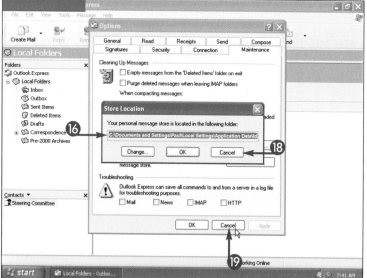

MOVE OLD MESSAGES FROM YOUR MESSAGE STORE

⑮ Follow Steps **1** to **4** in Task #74 to open the Store Location dialog box.

⑯ Select the folder text.

Note: To select the text quickly, click to the left of the first character and then press Shift+End.

⑰ Press Ctrl+C to copy the text.

⑱ Click Cancel.

⑲ Click Cancel.

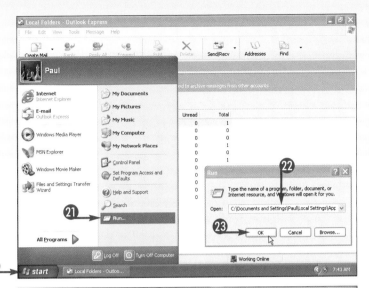

#75

CONTINUED

⑳ Click start.

㉑ Click Run.

The Run dialog box appears.

㉒ Press Ctrl+V to paste the message store folder location into the Open text box.

㉓ Click OK.

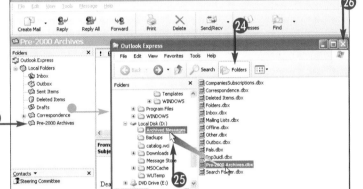

● Your message store folder appears.

㉔ Click Folders.

㉕ Click and drag the file representing your archived messages and drop it on the folder in which you want to store the archives.

㉖ Click here to close your message store folder.

㉗ In Outlook Express, click the archive folder.

㉘ Press Shift+Delete.

Outlook Express deletes the folder without storing it in the Deleted Items folder.

TIPS

Reverse It!

To get your archived messages back into Outlook Express, first re-create the folder that you used to store the messages. Click the folder to display it (this ensures that Outlook Express adds the folder to the message store) and then exit Outlook Express. Copy the archive file back into the message store folder. When Windows XP asks if you want to replace the existing file, click Yes. Restart Outlook Express. Your archived messages now appear in the folder.

Did You Know?

You can also use this task to move some or all of a message store to another computer. Use the previous tip to create a folder with the same name on the other computer. Copy the corresponding files from the original computer's message store and paste them to the other computer's message store. Click Yes when Windows XP asks if you want to replace the existing files.

CREATE A BACKUP COPY
of your address book

You can create a backup copy of your Address Book. If you have a problem with the Address Book in the future, you can restore your contacts from the backup copy.

The Windows XP Address Book is handy for storing e-mail addresses of people you correspond with regularly. Instead of remembering complex e-mail addresses, you simply type or select the person's name when composing a new message. However, the usefulness of the Address Book extends far beyond e-mail. For each contact, you can also store data

such as his or her home and business addresses, phone, fax, and cell numbers, spouse and children's names, gender, birthday, and more.

If you rely on the Address Book to store all this information about the people you know, then you must ensure that the data is safe. Unfortunately, the Address Book is just a single file on your hard drive, and if that file gets corrupted, you could lose all your contact data. Just in case this happens, you can regularly create backup copies of your Address Book, as described in this task.

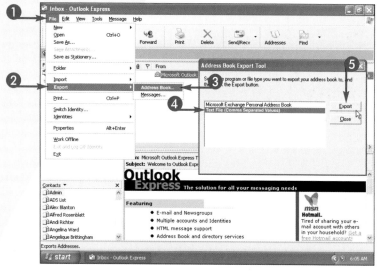

① In Outlook Express, click File.

② Click Export.

③ Click Address Book.

The Address Book Export Tool dialog box appears.

④ Click Text File (Comma Separated Values).

⑤ Click Export.

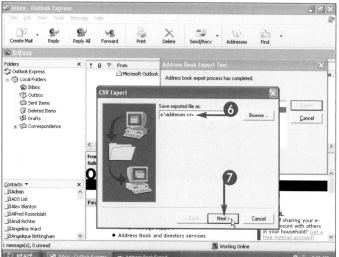

The CSV Export dialog box appears.

⑥ Type the location and name of the exported file.

*Note: Be sure to add **.csv** to the end of the exported filename.*

⑦ Click Next.

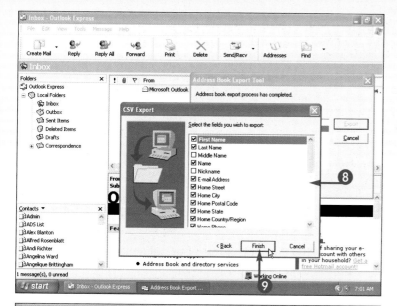

⑧ Click the check boxes for each field you want to include (☑) or exclude (☐).

⑨ Click Finish.

DIFFICULTY LEVEL

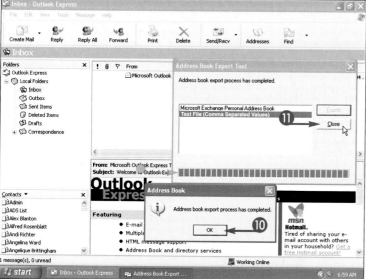

Outlook Express exports the Address Book data to the file.

● The progress of the export is shown here.

⑩ When the export is complete, click OK.

⑪ Click Close.

Important!

If you have a problem with your Address Book — for example, if it does not open or does not display your contacts — you can restore it by importing the backed-up copy. In Outlook Express, click File, Import, and then Other Address Book. Click Text File (Comma Separated Values), and then click Import. Type the location and name of the exported file from Step **6** and click Next. Click Finish.

Did You Know!

If you prefer to create a backup copy of the actual Address Book file, you must first discover the file's location. To do that, open the Address Book window and click Help and then About Address Book. Copy the folder name that appears, but do not include the Address Book filename — *User*.wab, where *User* is your Windows XP user name. Click start and then Run, paste the folder name, and click OK to open the Address Book folder. You can then copy the Address Book file to a backup location.

Identify
UNKNOWN SENDERS

If someone you do not know sends you a message, you can use one of the Internet's directory services to see if the sender is using a legitimate e-mail address.

Most of the e-mail messages you receive probably come from colleagues, friends, family members, and other people you know. However, you may receive the occasional message from an unknown sender. For example, many spam (unsolicited commercial e-mail) messages are sent via fake addresses so that the

sender cannot be traced. Also, messages with virus-infected files attached can sometimes come from illegitimate addresses.

If you are worried about a particular sender, Outlook Express has a feature that can help called Find People. You can use this feature to search for the sender's address using an Internet *directory service*, which is a kind of white pages directory for e-mail addresses. If the address exists in the directory, then you know that at least it is a legitimate address.

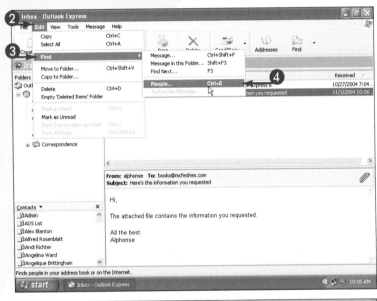

① Copy the sender's e-mail address, as described in the tip on the following page.

② Click Edit.

③ Click Find.

④ Click People.

Note: You can also press Ctrl+E.

The Find People dialog box appears.

⑤ Click here and then click a Directory Service item in the list.

⑥ Paste or type the sender's e-mail address.

⑦ Click Find Now.

Note: Make sure you are connected to the Internet before you click Find Now.

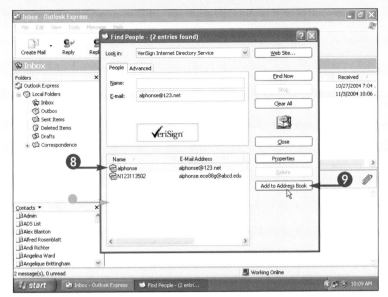

Outlook Express contacts the directory service and initiates the search for the address.

● If any entries are found, they appear here.

⑧ To add the sender to your Address Book, click the address.

⑨ Click Add to Address Book.

DIFFICULTY LEVEL

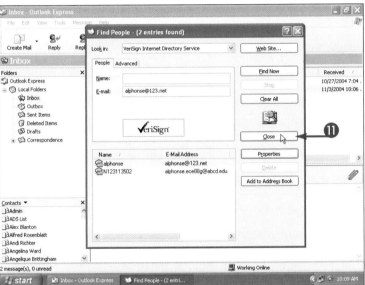

⑩ To try other directory services, repeat Steps **5** to **7**.

⑪ Click Close to close the Find People dialog box.

Exchange
ELECTRONIC BUSINESS CARDS

You can create an electronic version of a business card that includes your name, address, and contact information. You can then attach this business card to your messages, enabling other people to easily add you to their address books.

The ritual exchange of business cards is a common sight at meetings, conferences, and cocktail parties. With the advent of e-mail, however, fewer people are meeting face-to-face, so there are fewer opportunities to swap cards. Fortunately, Outlook Express offers a feature that enables you to

exchange business cards electronically. An electronic business card is called a *vCard* and, just like its paper counterpart, it includes the person's name, address, phone numbers, and other contact information. After you create a vCard for yourself, Outlook Express enables you to attach it to your messages. The recipient can then view the attached card and easily add you to his or her address book. Similarly, you can view vCards that are sent to you and add the senders to your Address Book.

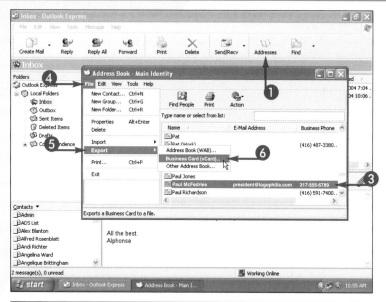

CREATE AN ELECTRONIC BUSINESS CARD

1️⃣ Click Addresses.

The Address Book window appears.

2️⃣ Create a new contact for yourself that includes the information that you want to appear in the electronic business card.

3️⃣ Click your name.

4️⃣ Click File.

5️⃣ Click Export.

6️⃣ Click Business Card (vCard).

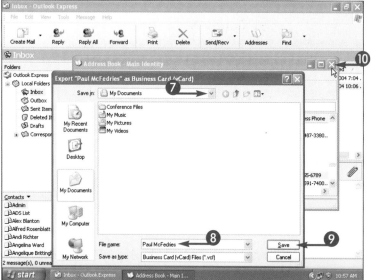

The Export dialog box appears.

7️⃣ Click here and then click the folder in which you want to store the business card.

8️⃣ Type the name you want to use.

9️⃣ Click Save.

🔟 Click here to close the Address Book window.

Outlook Express creates the vCard.

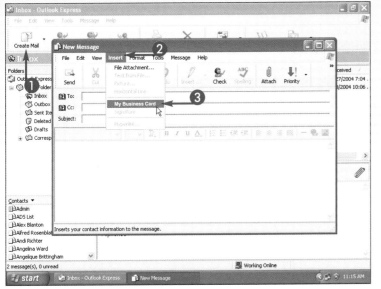

78

1. Click Create Mail to start a new message.

2. Click Insert.

3. Click My Business Card.

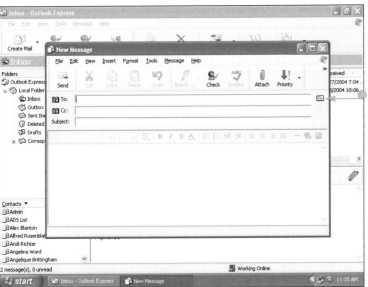

- Outlook Express adds the business card icon to the message.

  Note: If you decide not to attach the business card to your message, click Insert and then My Business Card.

Important!

If you cannot click the My Business Card command, click ☒ to return to Outlook Express. Click Tools, Options and then the Compose tab. In the Business Cards group, click Mail (☐ changes to ☑), click ☑ in the Mail list, and then click your name. If you do not want to include the vCard on all your messages, click Mail again (☑ changes to ☐). Click OK.

Did You Know?

If you receive a message that includes a vCard, you can see the business card icon in the preview pane. Click the icon and then click Open to open the attached vCard file. To add the sender to your Address Book, click Add to Address Book.

Chapter

9

Enhance Your Computer's Security and Privacy

These days you may be used to thinking that threats to your computer-related security and privacy only come from the Internet. That is not surprising because the very real threats of e-mail viruses, system intruders, and identity thieves receive the lion's share of press coverage.

However, many security experts believe that most violations of security and privacy occur not remotely, from the Internet, but locally, right at your computer. That is, computer security and privacy are comprised most often by someone simply sitting down at another person's machine while that person is not around. That makes some sense, because having physical access to a computer allows an intruder to install malicious programs, disable security features, and poke around for sensitive data such as passwords and credit card numbers.

If you are worried about having your security or privacy compromised by someone having direct access to your computer, Windows XP offers a reassuringly large number of tools and features that you can use to lock up your computer. In this chapter, you learn about most of these tools, many of which are quite simple to implement. Techniques such as adding a password to your account, putting your screen saver in security mode, and clearing your list of recently used documents and media files are all easy to set up, but provide greatly enhanced security and privacy. You also learn more advanced techniques that take security to the next level, including using advanced file permissions, encrypting files, and preventing other people from even starting your computer.

Top 100

ADD A PASSWORD
to your user account

You can configure your Windows XP user account with a password. Another person cannot log on to your account unless he or she knows the password.

Right out of the box, Windows XP is not very secure. In most cases, when you start your computer, you are taken directly to the Windows XP desktop. That may be convenient not only for you, but also for a system snoop who starts your machine while you are not around. With full access to the system, the snoop can install a virus, a Trojan horse — a program that

enables the hacker to control your computer from the Internet — or a program that monitors your keystrokes to grab your passwords. It is also easy for the intruder to root around in your files looking for sensitive information, or even to trash your precious data.

The first and most important step towards preventing all of this is to protect your user account with a password.

① Click start.

② Click Control Panel.

The Control Panel window appears.

③ Click User Accounts.

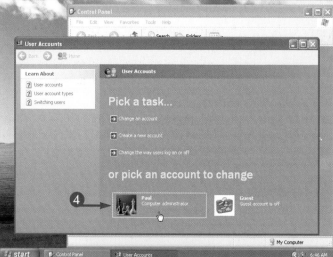

The User Accounts window appears.

④ Click the account to which you want to assign a password.

172

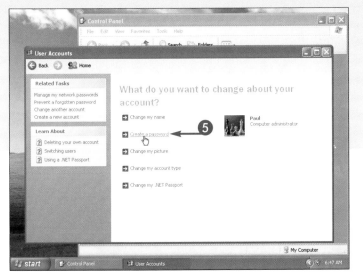

The What do you want to change about your account window appears.

5 Click Create a password.

The Create a password for your account window appears.

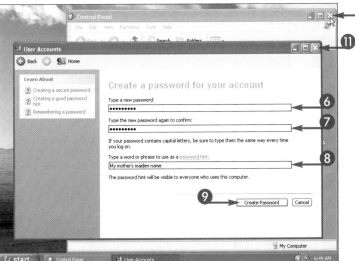

6 Type your password.

7 Type your password again.

8 Type a word or phrase as a hint.

9 Click Create Password.

10 When Windows XP asks if you want to make your files private, click Yes, Make Private.

11 Click here to close the User Accounts window.

12 Click here to close the Control Panel window.

Windows adds a password to your account.

Important!

When you choose a password, select one that nobody can guess, but one that you can remember. Here are some ideas:

● Do not use obvious passwords such as your name, the name of a family member or colleague, your birth date, or your Social Security number.

● Use a password that is at least eight characters long.

● Do not write down your password.

● Do not tell your password to anyone.

Important!

Here are more ideas for creating a strong password:

● Because Windows XP passwords are case-sensitive, mix uppercase and lowercase letters.

● Include numbers or punctuation marks in your password.

● Use a misspelled word.

● Use an acronym of a common phrase, such as the title of your favorite movie or book.

REQUIRE CTRL+ALT+DELETE
before logging on

You can configure Windows XP to require users to press Ctrl+Alt+Delete before they can log on to your computer. This prevents a malicious program activated at startup from capturing your password.

Protecting your Windows XP user account with a password (as described in Task #79), though an excellent idea, is not foolproof. Hackers are an endlessly resourceful bunch, and some of the smarter ones figured out a way to defeat the user account password system. The trick is that they install a virus or Trojan horse program — usually via an infected

e-mail message or malicious Web site — that loads itself when you start your computer. This program then displays a *fake* version of the Windows XP Log On to Windows dialog box. When you type your user name and password into this dialog box, the program records it and your system security is compromised.

To thwart this clever ruse, Windows XP enables you to configure your system so that you must press Ctrl+Alt+Delete before you can log on. This key combination ensures that the authentic Log On to Windows dialog box appears.

① Turn off the Windows XP Welcome screen, as described in the tip on the following page.

② Click start.

③ Click Run.

The Run dialog box appears.

④ In the Open text box, type **control userpasswords2**.

⑤ Click OK.

The User Accounts dialog box appears.

⑥ Click the Users tab.

⑦ Click Users must enter a user name and password to use this computer (☐ changes to ☑).

⑧ Click the Advanced tab.

⑨ Click Require users to press Ctrl+Alt+Delete (☐ changes to ☑).

⑩ Click OK.

Windows now requires each user to press Ctrl+Alt+Delete to log on.

TIPS

Important!

The Ctrl+Alt+Delete requirement only works if you disable the Windows XP Welcome screen and use the Log On to Windows dialog box instead. To disable the Welcome screen, click start, Control Panel, User Accounts, and then "Change the way users log on or off." Click Use the Welcome Screen (☑ changes to ☐), and then click Apply Options.

Did You Know?

When you are logged on to Windows XP, you can use Ctrl+Alt+Delete to change your user account password. Press Ctrl+Alt+Delete to display the Windows Security dialog box, and then click Change Password. Type your old password, your new password (twice), and then click OK.

Switch to
ADVANCED FILE PERMISSIONS

If you use Windows XP Professional, you can configure your file security to use advanced file permissions.

A computer with multiple users has its file security compromised in two ways. First, your My Documents folder is not secure because other Administrators can access it. Second, although Limited users cannot access your My Documents folder, they can access other folders on your computer.

To prevent the second problem, display the Sharing tab (right-click the folder you want secured and click Sharing and Security) and then click "Make this

folder private" (☐ changes to ☑). This is part of Windows XP's *simple file sharing*. Unfortunately, you cannot use simple file sharing to prevent Administrators from accessing your files. Also, you cannot set up simple file sharing to allow someone to view the files but not change them.

For these sophisticated security needs, you must turn off simple file sharing and use advanced file permissions instead. This gives you greater control over which users can access your shared files and what those users can do with those files (as described in Task #82).

① In Windows XP Professional, click start.

② Click Control Panel.

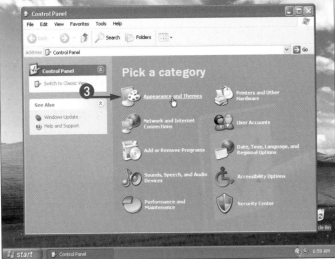

The Control Panel window appears.

③ Click Appearance and Themes.

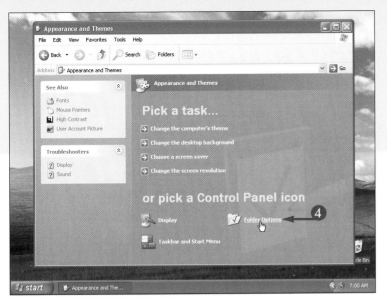

The Appearance and Themes window appears.

④ Click Folder Options.

81

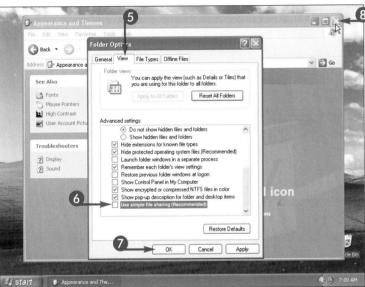

The Folder Options dialog box appears.

⑤ Click the View tab.

⑥ Click Use simple file sharing (☑ changes to ☐).

⑦ Click OK.

⑧ Click here to close the Appearance and Themes window.

Windows enables advanced file permissions.

Did You Know?

If you have a folder window open, a quicker way to get to the Folder Options dialog box is to click Tools and then Folder Options.

Important!

Simple file sharing is the only file security system available in Windows XP Home Edition. To use the advanced file permissions, you must have Windows XP Professional.

Important!

To use the advanced file permissions, your hard drive must use the NTFS file system. To convert a drive to NTFS, click start, All Programs, Accessories, Command Prompt. Type **convert *d*: /fs:ntfs**, where *d* is the letter of the hard drive you want to convert, and press Enter. If Windows XP asks to "dismount the volume," press Y and then Enter.

Protect your files with
ADVANCED FILE PERMISSIONS

You can use advanced file permissions to specify which users of your computer can access which folders, and what exactly those users can do with the files in those folders.

With simple file sharing turned off (see Task #81), Windows XP Professional offers a sophisticated file security system called *permissions*. Permissions specify exactly what the groups or users can do with the contents of the protected folder. There are six types of permissions:

Full Control — Users can perform any of the actions listed. Users can also change permissions.

Modify — Users can view the folder contents, open files, edit files, create new files and subfolders, delete files, and run programs.

Read and Execute — Users can view the folder contents, open files, and run programs.

List Folder Contents — Users can view the folder contents.

Read — Users can open files, but cannot edit them.

Write — Users can create new files and subfolders, and open and edit existing files.

In each case, you can either allow the permission or deny it.

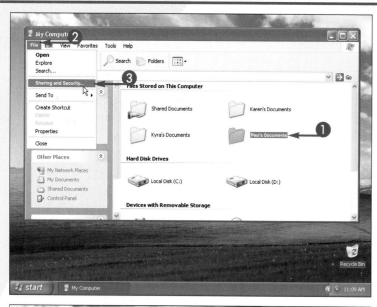

1 In a folder window, click the folder that you want to protect.

2 Click File.

3 Click Sharing and Security.

The folder's Properties dialog box appears.

4 Click the Security tab.

● This area lists the current groups and users that have permissions for the folder.

Note: The name in parentheses takes the form COMPUTER\Name, where COMPUTER is the computer's name and Name is the user or group name.

5 Click Add.

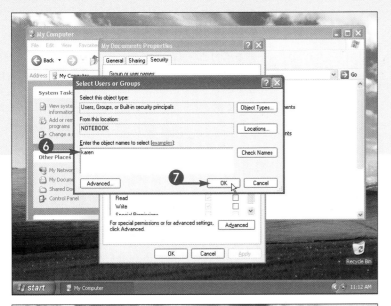

The Select Users or Groups dialog box appears.

⑥ Type the name of the group or user with which you want to work.

⑦ Click OK.

#82

DIFFICULTY LEVEL

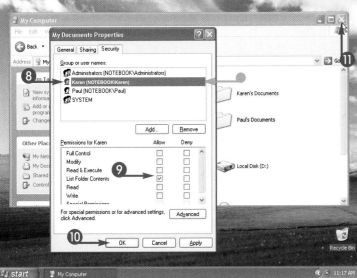

● The user or group appears in this list.

⑧ Click the new user or group to select it.

⑨ In the Allow column, click each permission that you want to allow (☑) or disallow (☐).

⑩ Click OK.

⑪ Click here to close the folder window.

Windows protects the folder with the permissions you selected.

TIPS

More Options!

In the Select Users or Groups dialog box, if you are not sure about a user or group name, click Advanced and then Find Now. Windows XP displays a list of all the available users and groups. Click the name you want in the list and then click OK.

More Options!

The permissions you choose may not work if the user inherits permissions from a group he or she is a member of (such as Administrators). In this case, you can override those permissions by clicking the corresponding check boxes in the Deny column (☐ changes to ☑). For example, to prevent a member of the Administrators group from viewing the contents of your folder, click List Folder Contents in the Deny column (☐ changes to ☑).

PROTECT
your shared network files

If you share files with other network users, you can configure Windows XP to control which users can access your files and what actions they can perform on those files.

If your computer is part of a network, it is common to give other users access to some of your files by sharing one or more folders with the network. To do this in most Windows XP systems, you display the Sharing tab (right-click the folder you want to share and click Sharing and Security) and then "Share this folder in the network" (☐ changes to ☑). This is

another aspect of the Windows XP simple file sharing feature described in Task #81. By default, Windows XP does not allow network users to change your files. If you want to give users the ability to edit shared files, you can also click "Allow network users to change my files" (☐ changes to ☑).

This is a crude mechanism because it gives *all* users the ability to change files. For better file security, you can apply permissions to shared network files as described in Task #82.

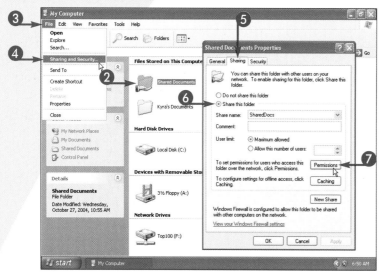

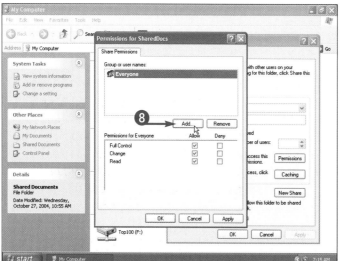

① Turn off simple file sharing (see Task #81).

② In a folder window, click the folder that you want to protect.

③ Click File.

④ Click Sharing and Security.

⑤ In the folder's Properties dialog box, click the Sharing tab.

⑥ Click Share this folder (○ changes to ⊙).

⑦ Click Permissions.

The shared folder's Permissions dialog box appears.

⑧ Click Add.

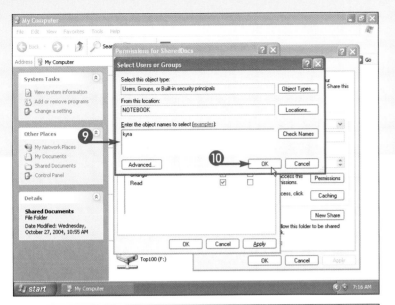

The Select Users or Groups dialog box appears.

⑨ Type the name of the group or user with which you want to work.

⑩ Click OK.

 # 83

DIFFICULTY LEVEL

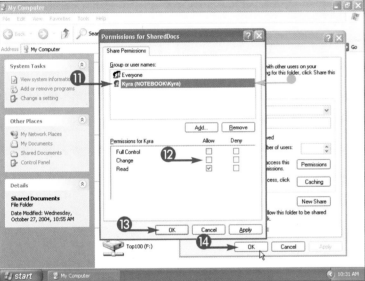

● The user or group appears in this list.

⑪ Click the new user or group to select it.

⑫ In the Allow column, click each permission that you want to allow (☑) or disallow (☐).

⑬ Click OK.

⑭ Click OK.

Windows shares the folder on the network and protects the folder with the permissions you selected.

Important!

If your computer is part of a workgroup, you can set up an account for each user on every computer in the workgroup. For example, if the user Paul has an account on computer A, you must also set up an account for Paul on computers B, C, and so on. You must assign a password to the account and you must use the same password for the account on all the computers.

More Options!

For a user who does not have an account on the local computer, Windows XP assigns the Guest account, which uses the permissions associated with the Everyone group. Therefore, you can control Guest access by setting permissions for the Everyone group. If you prefer that only users with local accounts access your shared resources, delete the Everyone group from the Permissions lists.

ENCRYPT
confidential files and folders

You can encrypt your most sensitive and confidential files so that no other person can read them.

Even if you have set up all the security mechanisms discussed in this chapter, it may still be possible for users to at least view your files. For example, hackers can use utilities to view the contents of your hard drive without logging on to Windows XP. That is not so much of a problem if what you are worried about is other people altering or deleting your files. However, it is a very big problem if your computer has files that contain extremely sensitive or

confidential information: personal financial files, medical histories, corporate salary data, trade secrets, business plans, and journals or diaries.

If you are worried about anyone viewing these or other for-your-eyes-only files, Windows XP Professional enables you to *encrypt* the file information. Encryption encodes the file so that it is completely unreadable by anyone unless they log on to your Windows XP account. After you encrypt your files, you work with them exactly as you did before, with no noticeable loss of performance.

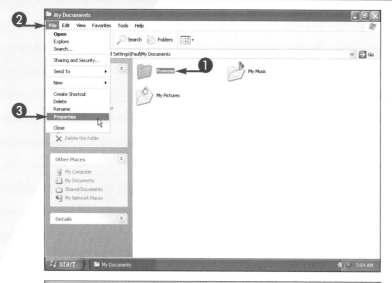

① In a folder window, click the folder containing the files that you want to encrypt.

Note: You can encrypt individual files, but encrypting an entire folder is easier. That way, Windows XP automatically encrypts new confidential files added to the folder.

② Click File.

③ Click Properties.

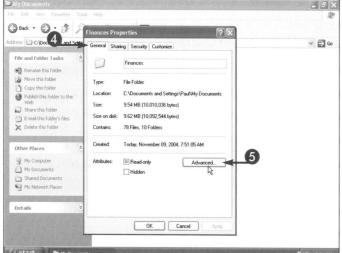

The folder's Properties dialog box appears.

④ Click the General tab.

⑤ Click Advanced.

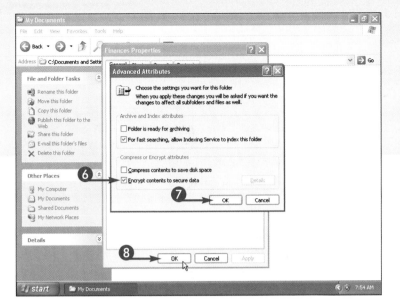

The Advanced Attributes dialog box appears.

84

⑥ Click Encrypt contents to secure data (☐ changes to ☑).

⑦ Click OK.

⑧ Click OK.

DIFFICULTY LEVEL

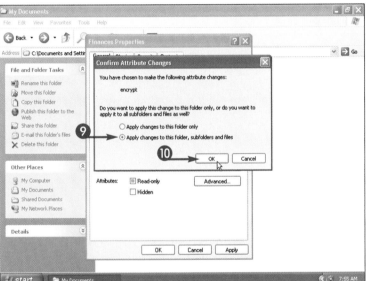

The Confirm Attribute Changes dialog box appears.

⑨ Click Apply changes to this folder, subfolders and file (○ changes to ◉).

⑩ Click OK.

Windows XP encrypts the folder's contents.

TIPS

Important!
File encryption is not supported by Windows XP Home Edition. To use file encryption, you must have Windows XP Professional.

Important!
To use file encryption, your hard drive must use NTFS (New Technology File System). To convert a drive to NTFS, see the tip in Task #81.

More Options!
If you want to give another user access to an encrypted file, first have that user log on and encrypt some of his or her own information. Log back on to your own account, click the file with which you want to work, and then click File and Properties. Click Details and then Add. Click the other user and then click OK.

PREVENT ACCESS
to your computer with a screen saver

You can use a screen saver to prevent another person from working with your computer while you are away from your desk.

Security measures such as advanced local file permissions (Tasks #81 and #82), advanced network file permissions (Task #83), and encryption (Task #84) all rely on the fact that you have entered the appropriate user name and password to log on to your Windows XP account. In other words, after you log on, you become a "trusted" user.

But what happens when you leave your desk? If you remain logged on to Windows XP, any other person who sits down at your computer can take advantage of your trusted-user status to view and work with secure files. You could prevent this by shutting down your computer every time you leave your desk, but that is not practical. A better solution is to configure your system with a password-protected screen saver. When someone deactivates the screen saver, he or she must enter your password to access the Windows XP desktop.

CONFIGURE THE SCREEN SAVER

1 Right-click the desktop.

2 Click Properties.

The Display Properties dialog box appears.

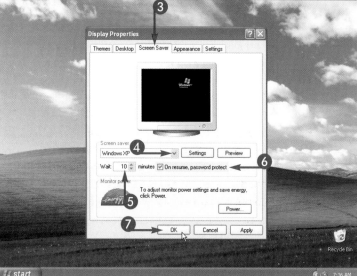

3 Click the Screen Saver tab.

4 Click here and then click the screen saver you want to use.

5 Type the number of minutes after which the screen saver activates.

6 Click On resume, password protect (☐ changes to ☑).

7 Click OK.

The next time the screen saver activates, your computer will be protected.

1 Press any key or move the mouse to deactivate the screen saver.

● The Computer Locked dialog box appears.

2 Press Ctrl+Alt+Delete.

DIFFICULTY LEVEL

The Unlock Computer dialog box appears.

Note: On some systems, you may see the Windows XP Welcome screen instead.

3 Type your password.

4 Click OK.

The Windows XP desktop appears.

Did You Know?

If your system does not work properly with a screen saver, you can also lock your computer by pressing the Windows Logo+L keys. Alternatively, press Ctrl+Alt+Delete and then click Lock Computer.

Try This!

If your screen saver kicks in while you are still at your desk, having to log on all over again can be a pain. You can prevent this with the Tweak UI PowerToy described in Task #91. Click Logon and then Screen Saver. Type a value, in seconds, in the box labeled "Grace period," and then click OK. The grace period is the number of seconds you have to deactivate the screen saver before the Computer Locked dialog box comes up.

PREVENT
others from starting your computer

You can configure Windows XP to require a special floppy disk to be inserted in your computer before starting up. Without the floppy disk, Windows XP does not allow anyone to log on to the computer.

As a security feature, Windows XP stores passwords in encrypted form. XP uses a *system key* to decrypt the passwords. This system key is normally stored on your computer, and if for some reason the system key were lost, you would not be able to start your computer. For this reason, the system key is also called a *startup key*.

You can take advantage of this security precaution to make sure that no unauthorized user can start your computer. You do that by having Windows XP move the startup key to a floppy disk. If the floppy disk is not inserted into the computer at startup, Windows XP does not allow anyone to log on to the system. In fact, Windows XP does not even display the Welcome screen or Log On dialog box, so an unauthorized user cannot even try to guess your password.

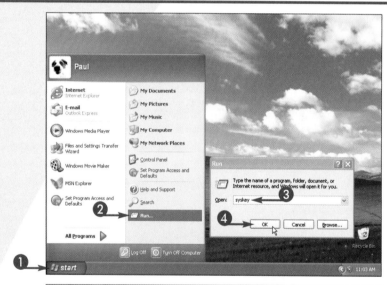

❶ Click start.

❷ Click Run.

The Run dialog box appears.

❸ Type **syskey**.

❹ Click OK.

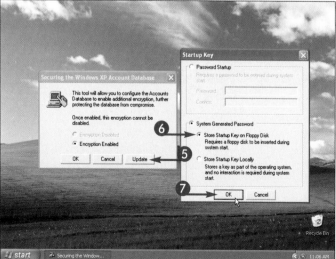

The Securing the Windows XP Account Database dialog box appears.

❺ Click Update.

The Startup Key dialog box appears.

❻ Click Store Startup Key on Floppy Disk (○ changes to ⊙).

❼ Click OK.

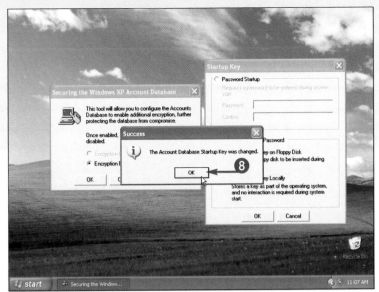

The Success dialog box appears.

⑧ Click OK

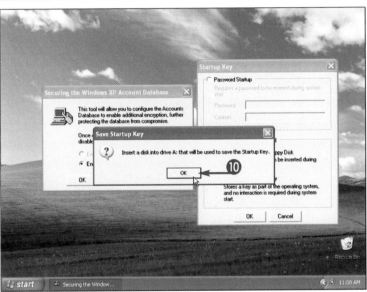

The Save Startup Key dialog box appears.

⑨ Insert a floppy disk into your computer's floppy disk drive.

⑩ Click OK.

Windows XP saves the startup key to the floppy disk and then displays a confirmation dialog box.

⑪ Click OK.

Windows now requires the floppy disk that contains the startup key to log on.

TIPS

Caution!

After saving the startup key to the floppy disk, Windows XP looks for the disk when you start your computer. If XP does not find the key, the Windows XP Startup Key Disk dialog box appears. You must insert the disk and then click OK. If you lose or damage the disk, you cannot start Windows XP, so keep the disk in a safe place. Also, be sure to make a backup copy of the disk.

Remove It!

If you decide later on that you no longer want to keep the startup key on a floppy disk, you can revert to storing the key on your computer. Follow Steps **1** to **5**, click Store Startup Key Locally (○ changes to ⊙), and then click OK.

Clear your list of
RECENTLY USED DOCUMENTS

For added privacy, you can clear the Start menu's My Recent Documents list so that other people who use your computer cannot see which documents you have been working on.

The Start menu's My Recent Documents list is handy because it enables you to quickly open the documents you use most often. However, if you know that someone else is going to be using your computer, and you do not have a separate user account set up for that person, you may not want him or her to see what is on your My Recent Documents list. To prevent this, you can clear the list.

TIP

Did You Know?

Many programs also maintain a list of the documents you have most recently opened. This list usually appears near the bottom of the File menu. You cannot always clear these lists, but in most cases you can, although the steps vary from programs to program. In Microsoft Word, for example, click Tools, Options, the General tab, and then "Recently used file list" (☑ changes to ☐).

① Right-click the start button.

② Click Properties.

The Taskbar and Start Menu Properties dialog box appears.

③ Click the Start Menu tab.

④ Click Customize.

The Customize Start Menu dialog box appears.

⑤ Click the Advanced tab.

⑥ Click Clear List.

Windows XP clears the My Recent Documents list.

⑦ Click OK.

⑧ Click OK.

Windows no longer lists your recently used documents.

Clear your list of
RECENTLY VIEWED MEDIA FILES

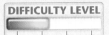

DIFFICULTY LEVEL

To enhance your privacy, you can clear the list of recently played media files maintained by Windows Media Player. This prevents other people who use your computer from seeing which media files you have recently opened.

In addition to maintaining a list of files that you have played recently, Windows Media Player also keeps track of the addresses of Internet media you have recently opened, as well as all the information you have downloaded about the audio CDs and DVDs you played. If someone else is going to use Windows Media Player on your computer, you can maintain your media privacy by clearing all this stored information.

Did You Know?

The easiest way to maintain the privacy of your documents is to create separate user accounts for each person who uses your computer. Click start, Control Panel, and then User Accounts. For maximum privacy, make everyone else a Limited user.

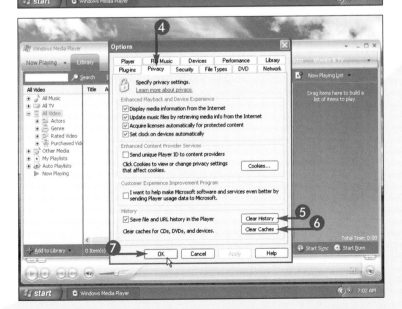

① In Windows Media Player, click the Access Application Menus button.

② Click Tools.

③ Click Options.

The Options dialog box appears.

④ Click the Privacy tab.

⑤ Click Clear History to clear the list of recently viewed media files and Internet addresses.

⑥ Click Clear Caches to clear the downloaded information about audio CDs and DVDs.

⑦ Click OK.

Windows Media Player no longer lists your recently used media files or Internet addresses.

PREVENT MALICIOUS CODE
from running

You can prevent damage from some types of malicious programming by activating a feature that stops those programs from running code in protected portions of your computer's memory.

Windows XP reserves some of your computer's memory as *system memory*, meant for use by Windows itself and by your programs. Windows reserves the rest of the memory for your open documents and other data. When programmers code software, they usually include fixed-size memory locations called *buffers* that hold data. Programs that require more data grab it from the hard drive and fill up the buffer.

Unfortunately, some poorly programmed software does not include a mechanism that watches for and prevents a *buffer overrun*: when a piece of data larger than the buffer size is loaded into the buffer. The extra data spills over into the system memory, resulting in system crashes. Some hackers use this flaw to deliberately crash or damage systems, or even to run malicious code. Windows XP Service Pack 2 includes a new feature called Data Execution Prevention (DEP) that prevents buffer overruns, and so protects your computer from these attacks.

① Click start.

② Right-click My Computer.

③ Click Properties.

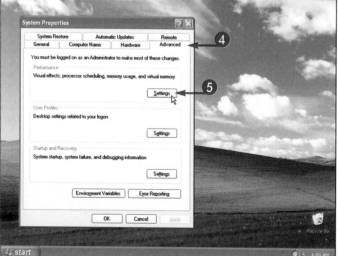

The System Properties dialog box appears.

④ Click the Advanced tab.

⑤ In the Performance group, click Settings.

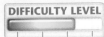

The Performance
Options dialog box
appears.

6 Click the Data
Execution Prevention
tab.

7 Click Turn on DEP for all
program and services
except those I select
(○ changes to ◉).

8 Click OK.

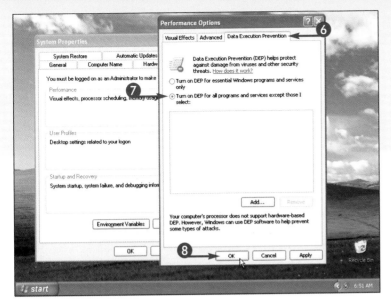

Windows XP warns you that you must
restart your computer to put the change
into effect.

9 Click OK.

10 Click OK.

11 Restart your computer.

Windows applies Data Execution
Prevention to all your programs.

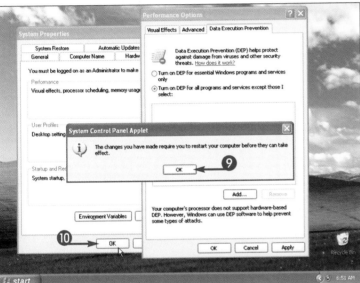

Important!

If Windows XP detects a system memory intrusion,
it shuts down the program that is causing the
problem and displays an error message. You should
immediately run a virus scan to ensure your
computer is not infected. Also, activate the
Windows Firewall, as described in Task #48. If there
is no virus and the firewall is on, the troublesome
program may not work if DEP is turned on. Contact
the software vendor to see if an updated version of
the malfunctioning program is available.

More Options!

If you have trouble running a program when DEP is
on, and your system is virus-free, running the
Windows Firewall, and no program update is
available, you can turn off DEP for that program.
Follow Steps 1 to 6 and then click Add. Use the
Open dialog box to display the program's folder,
click the executable file that runs the program, and
then click Open.

Extend Your System with PowerToys for Windows XP

Windows XP is a large, complex operating system with hundreds of programs, tools, services, and features. However, despite its size and complexity, Windows XP is not, nor could it ever be, in any sense a *complete* operating system. That is because we all use our computers in different ways and for different tasks, so there will always be tools or features that we wish were part of Windows XP but, alas, are not.

Some of the Windows XP programmers felt this lack, and luckily they have the skills to do something about it. They built a collection of programs and utilities called the PowerToys for Windows XP. There are 11 PowerToys in all, and they offer a wide range of new functions for Windows XP.

Some of the PowerToys extend or improve upon existing Windows XP features. For example, the Alt-Tab Replacement PowerToy

gives you a better version of the Alt+Tab method of switching from one program to another. Similarly, the PowerToy Calculator enables you to perform advanced mathematical calculations and even graph functions.

Some of the PowerToys give you new features that should probably be part of Windows XP. For example, the Image Resizer gives you an easy way to change the dimensions of an image. Then there is the Virtual Desktop Manager that enables you to manage up to four different desktop configurations, each with its own running programs and windows.

This chapter introduces you to all the PowerToys. First you learn how to download and install them, and then the rest of the tasks examine each PowerToy in turn.

Top 100

DOWNLOAD AND INSTALL
PowerToys

To use any PowerToy, you must first download it from Microsoft's Web site and then install it on your computer.

None of the 11 PowerToys are available either on the Windows XP CD or via a separate CD from Microsoft. Instead, they are all available as downloads on the Microsoft Web site. You must therefore have Internet access to get the PowerToys. If you do not have Internet access but you know someone who does, you could also ask that person to download each file to his or her hard drive, copy the downloaded files to

floppy disks or to a recordable CD, and then give you the disk.

Most of the PowerToys files are just a few hundred kilobytes, so even if you have a dial-up connection you can download each one in just a few minutes. From there, the installation process for each PowerToy is straightforward, and you rarely have to customize the installations in any way. Remember, too, that if you decide you no longer want to use a PowerToy, you can uninstall it by clicking start, Control Panel, and then Add or Remove Programs.

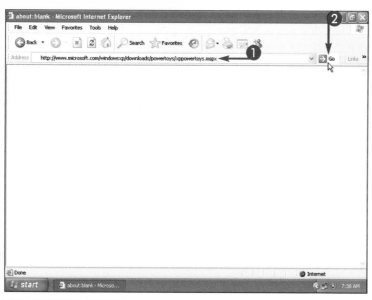

① In Internet Explorer, type the following address in the Address bar:

http://www.microsoft.com/ windowsxp/downloads/ powertoys/xppowertoys.mspx

② Click Go or press Enter.

The Microsoft PowerToys for Windows XP page appears.

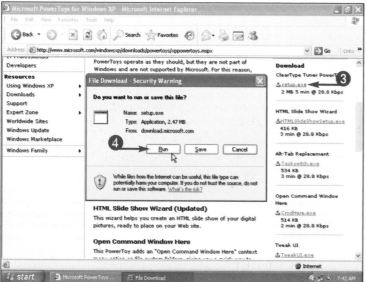

③ In the Download area, click the link for the PowerToy you want to install.

The File Download – Security Warning dialog box appears.

④ Click Run.

Windows XP downloads the PowerToy setup file.

When the download is complete, another Security Warning dialog box appears.

⑤ Click Run.

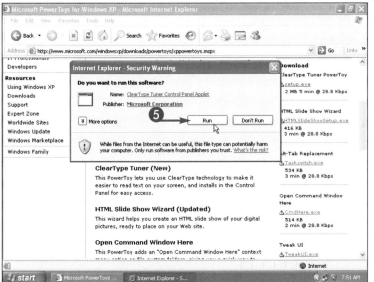

The PowerToy's installation wizard begins.

⑥ Click Next.

⑦ Follow the steps in the dialog boxes to install the PowerToy.

Note: Each PowerToy offers a slightly different installation process. However, each install is straightforward and consists of running through a few dialog boxes.

TIPS

Caution!

Although Microsoft makes the PowerToys for Windows XP available on its Web site, Microsoft does *not* support these programs. If you have problems running a PowerToy or if a PowerToy messes up your system, Microsoft will not help you. That said, all the PowerToys run well and you should not have any problems. If you do, uninstalling the PowerToy usually solves the problem.

Check It Out!

As this book went to press, Microsoft added the eleventh PowerToy: ClearType Tuner. This utility enhances your screen text by activating and optimizing Windows XP's built-in ClearType technology. ClearType Tuner makes your screen text dramatically clearer and easier to read, so this PowerToy is definitely worth the download.

Tweak Windows XP with
TWEAK UI

You can use the Tweak UI PowerToy to customize more than a dozen different Windows XP features and programs.

Tweak UI is by far the most versatile of the PowerToys. The purpose of this program is to give you an easy way to customize and tweak Windows XP. Tweak UI includes settings for features such as the taskbar and Start menu, dialog boxes, logging on, locations such as the Desktop, My Computer, and Control Panel, and programs such as Windows Explorer and Internet Explorer. It is certainly true that many of Tweak UI's settings are obscure and of little apparent benefit. But there are dozens of settings with which you can work, so Tweak UI is bound to have something that makes your Windows XP experience easier, faster, or more private.

This task shows you how to start and navigate the Tweak UI window. From there, you learn about many of Tweak UI's more useful settings, including how to customize Windows XP shortcuts. Feel free to browse through the Tweak UI settings to look for items that interest you. Go ahead and try them out, because all changes you make with Tweak UI are completely reversible.

START TWEAK UI

① Click start.

② Click All Programs.

③ Click Powertoys for Windows XP.

④ Click Tweak UI.

The Tweak UI window appears.

NAVIGATE TWEAK UI

- Tweak UI's features are arranged in a tree list.

- You can click ⊞ to open a branch and ⊟ to close an open branch.

- When you click a feature, its description or list of settings appear here.

- When you are done, you can click OK to put the new settings into effect.

- To put the settings into effect without closing Tweak UI, you can click Apply.

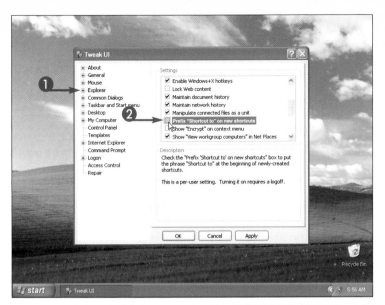

① Click Explorer.

② Click here (☑ changes to ☐) to eliminate "Shortcut to" on new shortcuts.

Note: You must log off Windows XP and then log back on to put this change into effect.

Note: See Task #1 to create shortcuts.

DIFFICULTY LEVEL

③ Click here to open the Explorer branch.

④ Click Shortcut.

⑤ Click the type of overlay image you want for all new shortcut icons (○ changes to ⊙).

● If you click the Custom option, you can click Change to choose the overlay image from the Change Icon dialog box (see Task #19).

TIPS

More Options!

Tasks #67 and #87 describe how to clear the Internet Explorer Address bar and the My Recent Documents list, respectively. To clear both lists automatically each time you exit Windows XP, click Explorer and then click the "Clear document history on exit" option (☐ changes to ☑).

More Options!

If you use the slide show feature (click "View as a slide show" in My Pictures), open the Explorer branch and click Slide Show. Use the "Time per picture" control to set the amount of time, in thousandths of a second, that each picture remains on-screen.

Tweak Windows XP with
TWEAK UI

You can also use Tweak UI to customize the Open and Save As dialog boxes, the Start menu, the taskbar, and Internet searching.

Windows XP has some common dialog boxes — such as Open and Save As — that programs from WordPad to Paint use. These common dialog boxes have a Places Bar on the left, which displays five icons for often-used folders, such as My Documents and the Desktop. Tweak UI enables you to customize the Places Bar to display your favorite folders.

For added privacy, Tweak UI also enables you to prevent programs from appearing on the Start menu's list of most frequently used programs.

When the taskbar gets full of buttons, Windows XP saves space by organizing multiple buttons from a single program into one button. Tweak UI enables you to control how Windows XP performs this grouping.

As described in Task #65, you can type **?** and then a term in the Internet Explorer Address bar to search for that term. The question mark (?) is called a *search prefix* and with Tweak UI you can create custom search prefixes for any other Internet search engine.

CUSTOMIZE THE PLACES BAR

● The Places Bar is shown here.

❶ Click here to open Common Dialogs.

❷ Click Places Bar.

❸ Click Custom places bar (○ changes to ⊙).

❹ In each list, click ⌄ and then click the location you want to appear in the Places Bar.

KEEP PROGRAMS OFF THE START MENU

❶ Click here to open the Taskbar and Start menu branch.

❷ Click Start Menu.

❸ Click the check box beside any program you want to keep off the Start menu (☑ changes to ☐).

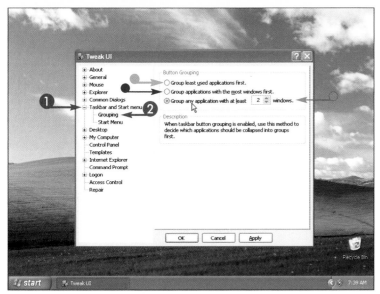

CONTROL TASKBAR GROUPING

① Click here to open the Taskbar and Start menu branch.

② Click Grouping.

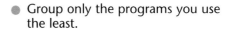

③ Choose a grouping option (○ changes to ◉).

● Group only the programs you use the least.

● Group only the programs with the most open windows.

● Group only those programs with at least the specified number of open windows.

CREATE INTERNET SEARCH PREFIXES

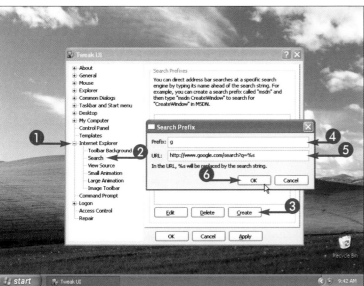

① Click here to open the Internet Explorer branch.

② Click Search.

③ Click Create.

④ In the Search Prefix dialog box, type the search prefix you want to use.

⑤ Type the address that the search engine uses to conduct searches. In the place where the search text appears, type **%s**.

⑥ Click OK.

TIPS

Did You Know?

Here are some search addresses you can enter in the Search Prefix dialog box:

AltaVista: http://www.altavista.com/cgi-bin/query?q=%s

AOL Search: http://search.aol.com/dirsearch.adp?from=msxp&query=%s

Ask Jeeves: http://www.askjeeves.com/main/askjeeves.asp?ask=%s

Google: http://www.google.com/search?q=%s

Did You Know?

Here are more search addresses you can enter in the Search Prefix dialog box:

Encarta (Dictionary): http://encarta.msn.com/encnet/features/dictionary/DictionaryResults.aspx?search=%s

Encarta (General): http://encarta.msn.com/encnet/refpages/search.aspx?q=%s

Excite: http://search.excite.com/search.gw?c=web&search=%s

Yahoo: http://search.yahoo.com/bin/search?p=%s

ALT-TAB REPLACEMENT

You can use the Alt-Tab Replacement PowerToy to make switching from one running program to another easier.

One of the first keyboard shortcuts mastered by almost all Windows users is Alt+Tab for switching programs. As you hold down Alt and press the Tab key, a small window of icons appears, one icon for each open program.

This works well, but the Alt+Tab window shows only the program icons and titles. The Alt-Tab Replacement PowerToy also shows you a copy of the entire program window, making it easier to select the one you want.

TIP

DIFFICULTY LEVEL

More Options!
Tweak UI (see Task #91) enables you to customize the normal Alt+Tab window. Open the General branch and click Alt+Tab. In the Rows text box, type the number of rows of icons you want to see in the Alt+Tab window. In the Columns text box, type the number of columns of icons you want to see in the Alt+Tab window.

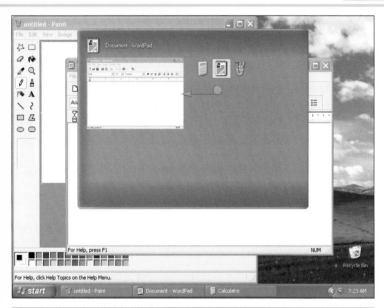

❶ Hold down the Alt key.

❷ Press Tab.

The Alt-Tab Replacement window appears.

● This part of the window shows a preview of the program you have currently selected.

❸ Press Tab.

● The preview window changes to the next running program.

❹ Repeat Step **3** until you see the program you want.

❹ Release Alt.

Windows XP switches to the program you selected.

COMMAND PROMPT

DIFFICULTY LEVEL

If you work with the command prompt, the Open Command Window Here PowerToy makes your life easier by enabling you to open the command prompt window in any folder you choose.

The command prompt (click start, All Programs, Accessories, and then Command Prompt) is occasionally useful for things like renaming multiple files in a folder. The Open Command Window Here PowerToy enables you to open the command prompt automatically in whatever folder you choose.

TIP

Did You Know?

The command prompt is useful when you want to rename multiple files in a folder. For example, if you download digital camera images, you may end up with files named dscn001.jpg, dscn002.jpg, and so on. To replace dscn with something more descriptive, use the REN (rename) command:
REN *OldName NewName*. Use **?** to substitute for single characters. Here is an example: **REN dscn???.jpg Picnic???.jpg**.

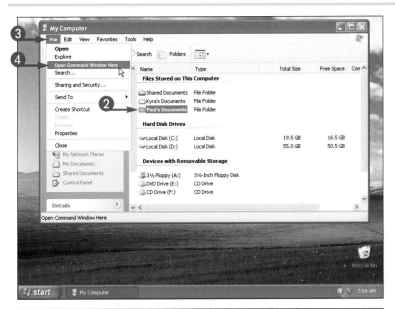

① Open the folder that contains the subfolder with which you want to work.

② Click the subfolder.

③ Click File.

④ Click Open Command Window Here.

The Command Prompt window appears.

● The command prompt displays the subfolder you selected.

Resize pictures with
IMAGE RESIZER

You can use the Image Resizer PowerToy to create copies of your images resized to whatever dimensions you specify. This is useful if you want to send the images to a Web site or another device that requires a certain image size.

Image files, particularly scans and digital photos, tend to be large. If you want to view images on a small device, such as a handheld PC, you must shrink the images so that they fit on a smaller screen. Similarly, uploading smaller images to a Web

site is always a good idea because they take less time for users to download and are easier to fit into your page design.

Task #23 describes a roundabout way to make images smaller by pretending to e-mail them. Unfortunately, Windows XP offers no direct way to change the size of any image. Fortunately, you can fill that gap with the Image Resizer PowerToy. This simple program enables you to create copies of your existing images sized to a standard dimension — such as the 240×320-pixel size that fits a handheld PC — or to whatever dimension you want.

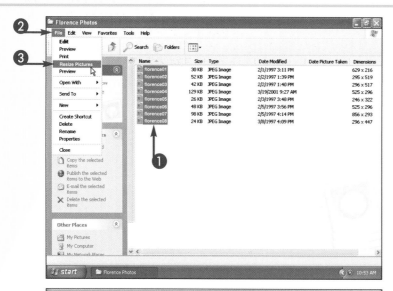

① Select the image files that you want to resize.

② Click File.

③ Click Resize Pictures.

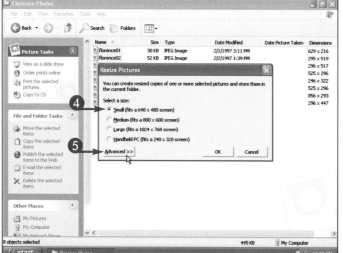

The Resize Pictures dialog box appears.

④ Click the image size you want (○ changes to ⊙).

⑤ Click Advanced.

The Resize Pictures dialog box expands to show more options.

202

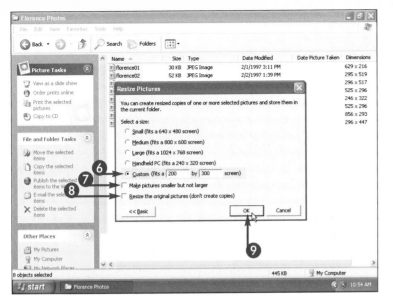

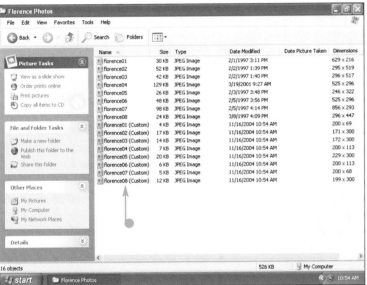

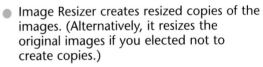

6 To specify your own image size, click here (○ changes to ◉) and type the width and height.

7 If an image is smaller than the size you selected, Image Resizer enlarges it. To prevent this, click here (□ changes to ☑).

8 To resize the images without making copies, click here (□ changes to ☑).

9 Click OK.

● Image Resizer creates resized copies of the images. (Alternatively, it resizes the original images if you elected not to create copies.)

Note: If you chose to make copies of the original images, the copies use the same names as the originals, with the type of size — Small, Medium, Custom, and so on — added in parentheses.

TIPS

Did You Know?

Image Resizer resizes a file to exactly the dimensions that you choose. To avoid distortion, the program maintains the image's *aspect ratio*: the ratio of the image's width to its height. For example, if the image's width is twice its length, then the width of the resized copy will also be twice its length. Image Resizer reduces (or enlarges) the image until both dimensions are less than or equal to the size you specified.

More Options!

Click on an image to see its dimensions. The dimensions appear in the status bar and in the Details pane. To see the dimensions for all your images, click View and then click Details.

VIEW MULTIPLE DESKTOPS
simultaneously

You can use the Virtual Desktop Manager PowerToy to configure up to four different desktops, each with its own set of open programs and documents. This helps to keep your screen uncluttered by showing only one or two windows in each desktop.

Windows XP's ability to *multitask* — run multiple programs at the same time — is a boon to productivity because it enables you to keep the programs you use most often open and ready for use. However, multitasking does have one major drawback: It makes your desktop a mess when you have a large number of windows open.

You can reclaim your desktop by using the Virtual Desktop Manager PowerToy. This program enables you to work with up to four different desktops, each of which can have its own set of program or document windows. For example, you may have your word processor open on one desktop, Outlook Express open on another, some Internet Explorer windows open on the third, and Windows Media Player running on the fourth. Virtual Desktop Manager makes switching between the desktops easy, and all the programs are available from any desktop, just in case you want to switch to one quickly.

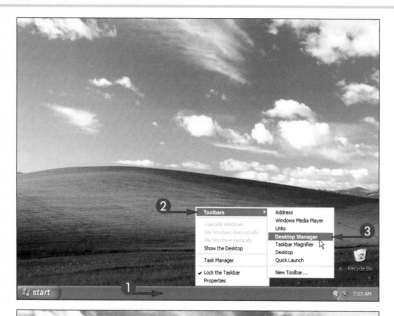

START VIRTUAL DESKTOP MANAGER

① Right-click an empty section of the taskbar.

② Click Toolbars.

③ Click Desktop Manager.

CONFIGURE DESKTOP PROGRAMS

● The Virtual Desktop Manager toolbar appears in the taskbar.

① Click the Quick Switch button for the desktop with which you want to work.

② Launch the program or programs that you want to appear on the desktop.

In this example, the desktop running WordPad is associated with Quick Switch button number 1.

③ Repeat Steps **1** to **2** for all the desktops you want to use.

PREVIEW THE DESKTOPS

1 Click the Preview button.

The Preview window appears, showing the four desktops.

DIFFICULTY LEVEL

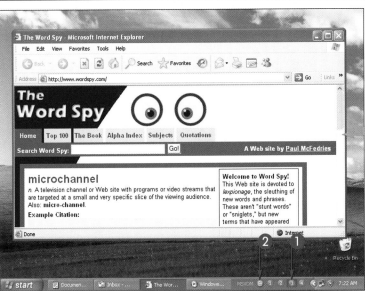

SWITCH TO ANOTHER DESKTOP

1 Click the desktop's Quick Switch button.

2 Click the Preview button to display the Preview window.

3 Click the desktop image.

● The desktop appears.

You can also hold down the Windows Logo key and press the number of the desktop. For example, press the Windows Logo+1 keys to switch to desktop 1.

TIPS

Remove It!

To turn off Virtual Desktop Manager, right-click an empty section of the taskbar, click Toolbars, and then click Desktop Manager.

More Options!

You can configure a separate background image for each desktop. Right-click MSVDM and then click Configure Desktop Images. Click the desktop with which you want to work and then use the Background list to click the image you want to use.

More Options!

To move a window to another desktop, display that desktop and then click the program's taskbar button. If you would rather restrict each window to its own desktop, right-click MSVDM and then click Shared Desktops.

Create a
CD SLIDE SHOW

With the CD Slide Show Generator PowerToy, you can transform a collection of images into an interactive, CD-based slide show. This is useful for sharing images with family, friends, or colleagues.

If you have a collection of digital photos, scans, drawings, or other images that you want to share, perhaps the biggest hurdle you face is how to distribute them. You could e-mail the images, but you may run into problems getting a number of large attachments past the recipient's service provider. You

could put the images on the Web, but that requires setting up — and possibly paying for — an account with a Web host and then building the site.

If you have a recordable CD drive, an attractive option is to put the images on a recordable CD and then give the disc to another person. CDs store up to about 650MB, so they can hold a large number of images. Even better, if you use the CD Slide Show Generator PowerToy, you can create an interactive slide show of the images for the recipient to enjoy.

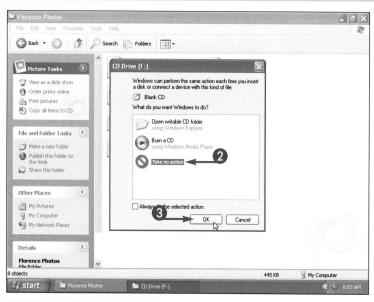

① Insert a recordable CD into your recordable CD drive.

A dialog box of options for the CD appears.

② Click Take no action.

③ Click OK.

④ Select the images you want to include in the CD slide show.

⑤ Click Copy to CD.

If you see the Confirm Stream Loss dialog box, click Yes each time it appears.

⑥ Repeat Steps 4 to 5 if you have images in other folders that you want to include in the CD slide show.

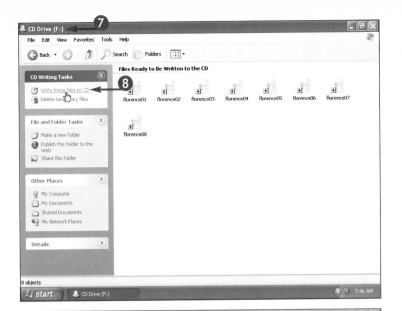

7 Display your recordable CD drive.

8 Click Write these files to CD.

DIFFICULTY LEVEL

The CD Writing Wizard appears.

9 Type a name for the recordable CD.

10 Click Next.

TIPS

Did You Know?

If you are recording a large number of images, it is possible you may exceed the 650MB limit for recordable CDs. To find out, display the recordable CD drive and select all the files in the section named Files Ready to Be Written to the CD. Click File and then Properties to display the Properties dialog box. The "Size on disk" number tells you the total size of the images.

Important!

For best results, start with an empty CD. Therefore, you can either use a new CD-R disc or erase a CD-RW disc. To erase a CD-RW disc, display the recordable CD and click File and then Erase this CD-RW. When the CD Writing Wizard appears, click Next.

Create a
CD SLIDE SHOW

Storing images on a CD is convenient, because a disc is easily transported or mailed. CDs are also durable (CD-based data maintains its integrity for many years) and safe (it is not easy to erase the contents of a CD).

Beyond that, the CD Slide Show Generator adds another benefit to the mix: ease of use for the recipient. The CD Slide Show Generator sets up the CD so that the recipient can start the slide show with

one mouse click. This is useful if you are sending the disc to a computer novice because the person does not have to perform a long or complex set of steps to start the show. Even better, although the slide show program added to the CD displays the slide show images automatically, the slide show is interactive; the recipient can pause the show, move backward and forward through the images, stop the show, and more.

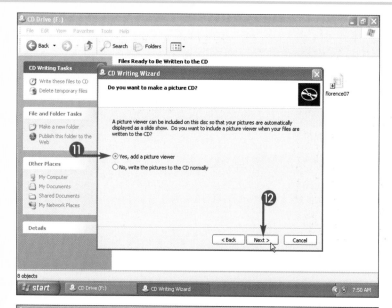

The Do you want to make a picture CD dialog box appears.

⑪ Click Yes, add a picture viewer (○ changes to ◉).

⑫ Click Next.

The CD Writing Wizard creates the CD slide show.

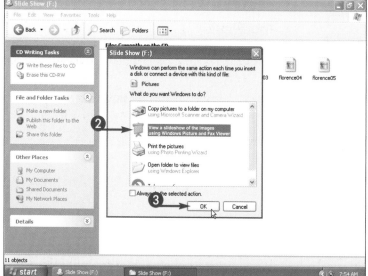

VIEW THE CD SLIDE SHOW

① Insert the slide show CD into a CD drive.

A dialog box of options for the CD appears.

② Click View a slideshow of the images using Windows Picture and Fax Viewer.

③ Click OK.

The CD slide show begins.

● You can move the mouse to display the slide show controls.

● You can click these buttons to control the slide show:

⏸ Pause the slide show

▶ Resume the slide show

⏮ View the previous picture

⏭ View the next picture

⏹ Stop the slide show

TIPS

More Options!

Use the following techniques to control the slide show via the keyboard:

● To pause the show, display the controls and press Tab to select ⏸.
● To restart the show, display the controls and press the space bar.
● To display the previous slide, press the down arrow key.
● To display the next slide, press the up arrow key.
● To stop the slide show, press the Escape key.

Did You Know?

If you stop the slide show and want to restart it, display the recordable CD drive and double-click the autorun file shown here.

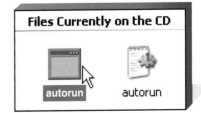

Create a Web page
SLIDE SHOW

One way you can share images with other people is by creating a slide show on your Web site. This makes the images available to anyone who has Internet access.

The CD Slide Show Generator PowerToy described in Task #96 is an excellent tool for sharing images with friends, family, and colleagues who do not have Internet access, or if you do not want to set up and maintain a Web site. However, most people do have Internet accounts these days, and plenty of free Web

hosting providers are still available. Therefore, the easiest and most convenient way to share pictures is usually by putting them on the Web.

Unfortunately, configuring Web pages by hand to show your images can be time-consuming. You can avoid that hassle by using the HTML Slide Show Wizard PowerToy. This wizard takes you step-by-step through the process of selecting and configuring images. It then creates the Web pages automatically, so all you have to do is upload them to your site.

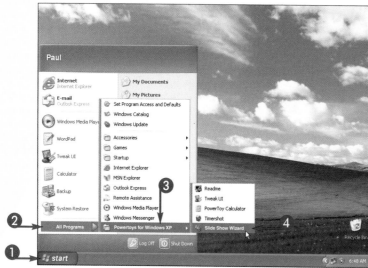

① Click start.

② Click All Programs.

③ Click Powertoys for Windows XP.

④ Click Slide Show Wizard.

The Slide Show Wizard appears.

⑤ Click Next.

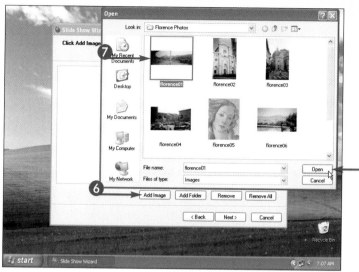

The next Slide Show Wizard dialog box appears.

6 Click Add Image.

The Open dialog box appears.

7 Click the image you want to include in the slide show.

8 Click Open.

9 Repeat Steps **7** to **8** for any other images you want to include in the slide show.

● The images you select appear in the Slide Show Wizard dialog box.

10 Click Next.

TIPS

Did You Know?
In the Open dialog box, you can use the following techniques to select multiple images:
● To select consecutive images, click the first image, hold down the Shift key and click the last image that you want.
● To select random images, hold down the Ctrl key and click each image you want.
● To select all the images, press Ctrl+A.

Change It!
After you have all your images displayed in the Slide Show Wizard, you can change their order as needed. To move an image, click and drag the image to the position you prefer. You can also remove an image: Click the image and then click Remove.

Create a Web page
SLIDE SHOW

The Slide Show Wizard creates a new folder called My Slide Shows in your My Documents folder. Within My Slide Shows you see another folder with the name you typed for your slide show. For example, if you named your slide show Vacation Pictures, you see a folder named Vacation Pictures within My Slide Shows.

The slide show folder contains all the data you need to upload to your Web site so that people can see the show. The Web page file named default.htm serves

as the "home page" for the slide show. There are also two folders — html and images — that you must upload in their entirety. (Upload the folders themselves, not just their contents.)

Uploading these files to your main Web directory may cause problems with existing files; instead, create a new folder on your Web site to hold the slide show files.

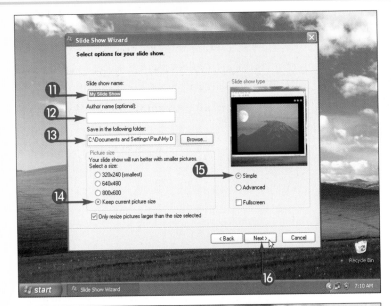

The next Slide Show Wizard dialog box appears.

⑪ Type a name for your slide show.

⑫ Type your name.

⑬ Choose the folder in which you want to save the slide show.

⑭ Click a picture size (○ changes to ◉).

⑮ Click a slide show type (○ changes to ◉).

⑯ Click Next.

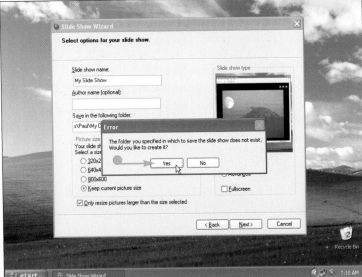

If the folder to which you are saving the slide show does not exist, the Error dialog box appears.

● You can click Yes to create a folder.

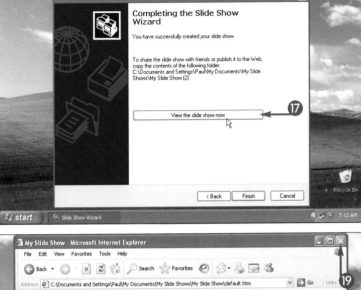

The final Slide Show Wizard dialog box appears.

⑰ To test the slide show, click View the slide show now.

The slide show opens in Internet Explorer.

● If the Information Bar appears, click it, click Allow Blocked Content, and then click Yes.

⑱ Click here to begin the slide show.

⑲ When the slide show finishes, click here to close the window.

⑳ Click Finish to complete the Slide Show Wizard.

㉑ Upload the slide show files to your Web site.

TIPS

More Options!
Use the following techniques to control the slide show:

● To display the next slide, click ▐◗.
● To display the previous slide, click ◖▐.
● To display the slide show images automatically, click ▶.
● To pause the slide show, click ▐▐.

Did You Know?
The Advanced slide show type displays the same controls as the Simple slide show, but it also provides three extra links: the Slide Show link runs the slide show; the Filmstrip link shows the current image with smaller versions of the other images underneath (like the Filmstrip view in the My Pictures folder); and the Previews link shows smaller versions of each slide show image.

Magnify your screen with
TASKBAR MAGNIFIER

If you are visually impaired, or if your eyesight is not what it once was, you can use the Taskbar Magnifier PowerToy to zoom in on a portion of the screen.

Windows XP's tiny type and small icons are hard to read for anyone whose eyesight is not 20/20. If you have a visual impairment or are experiencing the visual degeneration that comes with age, the Taskbar Magnifier can help. This PowerToy displays a magnified view of whatever part of the screen you are using, making even the smallest text and icons easy to see.

DIFFICULTY LEVEL

More Options!
To change the magnification, right-click the Taskbar Magnifier, click Zoom, and then click the magnification you want.

Reverse It!
To turn off the Taskbar Magnifier, right-click an empty section of the taskbar, click Toolbars, and then click Taskbar Magnifier.

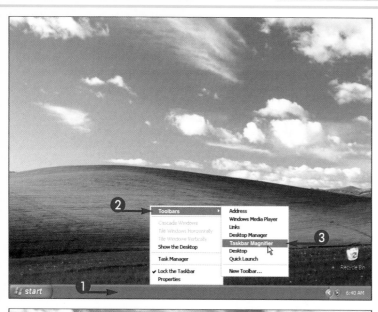

❶ Right-click an empty section of the taskbar.

❷ Click Toolbars.

❸ Click Taskbar Magnifier.

● The Taskbar Magnifier appears.

❹ Position the mouse over a screen element.

● The screen element appears magnified here.

ADVANCED CALCULATIONS #99

If you have serious calculation needs, forget the Windows XP Calculator and turn instead to the advanced PowerToy Calculator.

PowerToy Calculator is a calculator program that goes well beyond the usual addition, subtraction, multiplication, and division. It has built-in conversion functions for converting between standard and metric values for length, mass, velocity, and temperature; it supports all trig and log functions; it supports the constants pi and e; it enables you to create your own variables; and it enables you to create and even graph your own functions.

DIFFICULTY LEVEL

More Options!
To convert a numeric value, type the number in the Input box, click Conversions, the category (such as Length), the subcategory (such as yard), and then click the conversion (such as meter). Press Enter to see the result.

More Options!
To access the trig and log functions, click Functions and then click either Trig Functions or Log Functions.

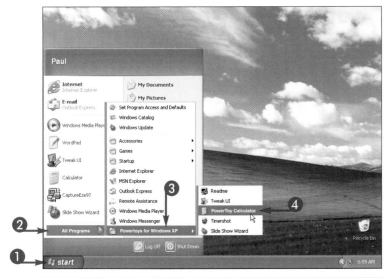

① Click start.

② Click All Programs.

③ Click Powertoys for Windows XP.

④ Click PowerToy Calculator.

The PowerToy Calc window appears.

⑤ Use the Input box to type your calculation, variable assignment, or function.

⑥ Press Enter.

● The calculation result appears here.

● You can double-click a constant to add it to the Input box.

● Your variable assignments appear here.

TAKE WEBCAM PICTURES
at regular intervals

The Timershot PowerToy enables you to take a picture at a specified interval from a Web cam or other desktop camera and save the image to your hard drive. This is useful if you want to take pictures of a scene at regular intervals.

Many Web or network sites are set up to show an image of a particular place or thing, where the image is updated at regular intervals. The first such "Web cam" was set up by programmers to show a coffee

station on another floor of the building where they worked, because they wanted to know when a fresh pot had been brewed.

Putting images on the Web or in a network folder is not difficult, but to receive images at regular intervals requires special software. You can get such software free by using the Webcam Timershot PowerToy. This program uses a desktop camera to take pictures at regular intervals. You can save those pictures to your own computer or to a Web site, FTP site, or network folder.

1 Click start.

2 Click All Programs.

3 Click Powertoys for Windows XP.

4 Click Timershot.

The Timershot window appears.

● You can click here to take a picture.

● You can click here to see the last picture taken.

5 Click here to expand the window.

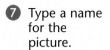

6 Use these controls to set how often Timershot takes a picture.

7 Type a name for the picture.

8 To change the location of the saved picture, click Browse and navigate to the folder.

9 Click Close Window to remove the Timershot window from the desktop.

Note: Timershot is still active and will take pictures at the interval you specified.

SHUT DOWN TIMERSHOT

Note: While the Timershot program is running, a Timershot icon appears in the taskbar's notification area.

1 Right-click the Timershot icon.

2 Click Exit.

Windows shuts down Timershot.

TIPS

More Options!

If you want to monitor an area over a period of time, click "Save a new copy of this file every time a picture is taken" (☐ changes to ☑). This creates a series of pictures that you can examine later on.

More Options!

To save pictures to a Web or FTP site, click Add Network Place Wizard and follow the dialog boxes to create a network place for the site. Then click Browse and choose the new network place as the Save In location.

Appendix
Windows XP Keyboard Shortcuts

Windows XP was made with the mouse in mind, so most day-to-day tasks are designed to be performed using the standard mouse moves. However, this does not mean your keyboard should be ignored when you are not typing. Windows XP is loaded with keyboard shortcuts and techniques that can often be used as replacements or enhancements for mouse clicks and drags. These shortcuts are often a faster way to work because you do not have to move your hand from the keyboard to the mouse and back. Also, the Windows XP keyboard techniques are useful to know just in case you have problems with your mouse and must rely on the keyboard to get your work done.

This bonus appendix consolidates all the Windows XP shortcut keys and techniques in one place for handy reference.

General Windows XP Shortcut Keys	
Press	*To do this*
Ctrl+Esc	Open the Start menu
Windows Logo	Open the Start menu
Ctrl+Alt+Delete	Display the Windows Security dialog box
Print Screen	Copy the entire screen image to memory
Alt+Print Screen	Copy the active window's image to memory
Alt+Double-click	Display the Properties dialog box for the selected item
Alt+Enter	Display the Properties dialog box for the selected object
Shift	Prevent an inserted CD from running its AutoPlay application by holding down Shift while inserting the CD
Shift+F10	Display the shortcut menu for the selected object — the same as right-clicking the object
Shift+Right-click	Display the shortcut menu with alternative commands for the selected object

Shortcut Keys for Working with Program Windows	
Press	*To do this*
Alt	Activate or deactivate the program's menu bar
Alt+Esc	Cycle through the open program windows
Alt+F4	Close the active program window
Alt+Spacebar	Display the system menu for the active program window
Alt+Tab	Cycle through icons for each of the running programs
F1	Display context-sensitive Help
F10	Activate the application's menu bar

Shortcut Keys for Working with Documents

Press	To do this
Alt+-(hyphen)	Display the system menu for the active document window
Alt+Print Screen	Copy the active window's image to the Clipboard
Ctrl+F4	Close the active document window
Ctrl+F6	Cycle through the open documents within an application
Ctrl+N	Create a new document
Ctrl+O	Display the Open dialog box
Ctrl+P	Display the Print dialog box
Ctrl+S	Save the current file If the file is new, display the Save As dialog box

Shortcut Keys for Working with Data

Press	To do this
Backspace	Delete the character to the left of the insertion point
Ctrl+C	Copy the selected data to memory
Ctrl+F	Display the Find dialog box
Ctrl+H	Display the Replace dialog box
Ctrl+X	Cut the selected data to memory
Ctrl+V	Paste the most recently cut or copied data from memory
Ctrl+Z	Undo the most recent action
Delete	Delete the selected data
F3	Repeat the most recent Find operation

Shortcut Keys for Moving the Insertion Point

Press	To do this
Ctrl+End	Move the insertion point to the end of the document
Ctrl+Home	Move the insertion point to the beginning of the document
Ctrl+Left Arrow	Move the insertion point to the next word to the left
Ctrl+Right Arrow	Move the insertion point to the next word to the right
Ctrl+Down Arrow	Move the insertion point to the end of the paragraph
Ctrl+Up Arrow	Move the insertion point to the beginning of the paragraph

Shortcut Keys for Selecting Text

Press	To do this
Ctrl+A	Select all the text in the current document
Ctrl+Shift+End	Select from the insertion point to the end of the document
Ctrl+Shift+Home	Select from the insertion point to the beginning of the document
Ctrl+Shift+Left Arrow	Select the next word to the left
Ctrl+Shift+Right Arrow	Select the next word to the right
Ctrl+Shift+Down Arrow	Select from the insertion point to the end of the paragraph
Ctrl+Shift+Up Arrow	Select from the insertion point to the beginning of the paragraph
Shift+End	Select from the insertion point to the end of the line
Shift+Home	Select from the insertion point to the beginning of the line
Shift+Left Arrow	Select the next character to the left
Shift+Right Arrow	Select the next character to the right
Shift+Down Arrow	Select the next line down
Shift+Up Arrow	Select the next line up

Shortcut Keys for Working with Dialog Boxes

Press	To do this
Alt+Down Arrow	Display the list in a drop-down list box
Alt+*Underlined letter*	Select a control
Ctrl+Shift+Tab	Move backward through the dialog box tabs
Ctrl+Tab	Move forward through the dialog box tabs
Enter	Select the default command button or the active command button
Spacebar	Toggle a check box on and off; select the active option button or command button
Esc	Close the dialog box without making any changes
F1	Display Help text for the control that has the focus
F4	Display the list in a drop-down list box
Backspace	In the Open and Save As dialog boxes, move up to the parent folder when the folder list has the focus
Shift+Tab	Move backward through the dialog box controls
Tab	Move forward through the dialog box controls

Shortcut Keys for Drag-and-Drop

Hold down	To do this
Ctrl	Copy the dragged object
Ctrl+Shift	Display a shortcut menu after dropping a left-dragged object
Esc	Cancel the current drag
Shift	Move the dragged object

Shortcut Keys for Working in a Folder Window

Press	To do this
Alt+Left Arrow	Navigate backward to a previously displayed folder
Alt+Right Arrow	Navigate forward to a previously displayed folder
Backspace	Navigate to the parent folder of the current folder
Ctrl+A	Select all the objects in the current folder
Ctrl+C	Copy the selected objects
Ctrl+V	Paste the most recently cut or copied objects
Ctrl+X	Cut the selected objects
Ctrl+Z	Undo the most recent action
Delete	Delete the selected objects
F2	Rename the selected object
F3	Display the Search Companion
F5	Refresh the folder contents
Shift+Delete	Delete the currently selected objects without sending them to the Recycle Bin

Shortcut Keys for Working with Internet Explorer

Press	To do this
Alt+Home	Go to the home page
Alt+Left Arrow	Navigate backward to a previously displayed Web page
Alt+Right Arrow	Navigate forward to a previously displayed Web page
Ctrl+A	Select the entire Web page
	Continued

Shortcut Keys for Working with Internet Explorer *(continued)*

Press	To do this
Ctrl+B	Display the Organize Favorites dialog box
Ctrl+D	Add the current page to the Favorites list
Ctrl+E	Display the Search Companion Explorer Bar
Ctrl+F	Display the Find dialog box
Ctrl+H	Display the History list Explorer Bar
Ctrl+I	Display the Favorites list Explorer Bar
Ctrl+N	Open a new window
Ctrl+O	Display the Open dialog box
Ctrl+P	Display the Print dialog box
Ctrl+Shift+Tab	Cycle backward through the Web page frames and the Address toolbar
Ctrl+Tab	Cycle forward through the Web page frames and the Address toolbar
Esc	Stop downloading the Web page
F4	Open the Address toolbar's drop-down list
F5	Refresh the Web page
F11	Toggle between Full Screen mode and the regular window
Spacebar	Scroll down one screen
Shift+Spacebar	Scroll up one screen
Shift+Tab	Cycle backward through the Address toolbar and the Web page links
Tab	Cycle forward through the Web page links and the Address toolbar

Shortcut Keys for Working with Windows Media Player

Press	To do this
Ctrl+P	Play or pause the current media
Ctrl+S	Stop the current media
Ctrl+B	Go to the previous track
Ctrl+Shift+B	Rewind to the beginning of the media
Ctrl+F	Go to the next track
Ctrl+Shift+F	Fast-forward to the end of the media
Ctrl+H	Toggle Shuffle playback
Ctrl+T	Toggle Repeat playback

Continued

Shortcut Keys for Working with Windows Media Player *(continued)*

Press	To do this
Ctrl+M	Show the menu bar
Ctrl+Shift+M	Autohide the menu bar
Ctrl+1	Switch to Full mode
Ctrl+2	Switch to Skin mode
F8	Mute sound
F9	Decrease volume
F10	Increase volume

Windows Logo key Shortcut Keys

Press	To do this
Windows Logo	Open the Start menu
Windows Logo+D	Minimize all open windows Press Windows Logo+D again to restore the windows
Windows Logo+E	Open Windows Explorer
Windows Logo+F	Display the Search Companion
Windows Logo+Ctrl+F	Find a computer
Windows Logo+L	Lock the computer
Windows Logo+M	Minimize all open windows
Windows Logo+Shift+M	Undo minimize all
Windows Logo+R	Display the Run dialog box
Windows Logo+U	Display the Utility Manager
Windows Logo+F1	Display Windows Help
Windows Logo+Break	Display the System Properties dialog box
Windows Logo+Spacebar	Scroll down one page (supported only in certain applications, such as Internet Explorer)
Windows Logo+Shift+Spacebar	Scroll up one page (supported only in certain applications, such as Internet Explorer)
Windows Logo+Tab	Cycle through the taskbar buttons

INDEX

INDEX

INDEX